S0-BYJ-878

Cold Noses and
Warm Hearts

Cold Noses and
Warm Hearts

Beloved Dog Stories
by Great Authors

Compiled, introduced, and revised
by Laurie Morrow
from the original edition

Willow Creek Press

© 2006 by Laurie Morrow

Illustrations by Christopher Smith

Hardcover first published in 1996 by Willow Creek Press
P.O. Box 147, Minocqua, Wisconsin 54548

Revised from Corey Ford's collection of dog stories
published with the same title in 1959.

All rights reserved. No part of this book may be reproduced or
transmitted in any form by any means, electronic or mechanical,
including photocopying, recording, or by any information storage and
retrieval system, without permission in writing from the Publisher.

Library of Congress Cataloging-in-Publication Data

Cold noses and warm hearts : beloved dog stories by great authors /
   compiled, introduced, and revised by Laurie Morrow from the original
   edition.

      p. cm.
   A revised ed. of Corey Ford's collection of dog stories published in
1959 under the same title.
      ISBN 1-59543-441-0 (alk. paper)
      1. Dogs--United States--Anecdotes.   2. Authors, American--
Anecdotes.   3. Dog owners--United States--Anecdotes.   4. Dogs--
Anecdotes.   5. Authors--Anecdotes.   6. Dog owners--Anecdotes.
I. Morrow, Laurie
SF426.2.C65   1996
813'.5408036--dc20   96-41386
                                                                    CIP

Printed in the U.S.A.

For my writing partner, mentor, and friend across the miles and the years, outdoor writer and field dog magazine editor Steve Smith

The Power of the Dog

There is sorrow enough in the natural way
From men and women to fill our day;
And when we are certain of sorrow in store,
Why do we always arrange for more?
Brothers and Sisters, I bid you beware
Of giving your heart to a dog to tear.

Buy a pup and your money will buy
Love unflinching that cannot lie—
Perfect passion and worship fed
By a kick in the ribs or a pat on the head.
Nevertheless it is hardly fair
To risk your heart for a dog to tear.

When the fourteen years which Nature permits
Are closing in asthma, or tumor, or fits,
And the vet's unspoken prescription runs
To lethal chambers or loaded guns,
Then you will find—it's your own affair—
But... you've given your heart to a dog to tear.

When the body that lived at your single will,
With its whimper of welcome, it stilled (how still!)
When the spirit that answered your every mood
Is gone—wherever it goes—for good
You will discover how much you care,
And will give your heart to a dog to tear.

We've sorrow enough in the natural way,
When it comes to burying in Christian clay.
Our loves are not given, but only lent,
At compound interest of cent per cent.
Though it is not always the case, I believe,
That the longer we've kept 'em, the more do we grieve.

For, when debts are payable, right or wrong,
A short time loan is as bad as a long—
So why in—Heaven (before we are there)
Should we give our hearts to a dog to tear?

—Rudyard Kipling

Contents

Introduction

Cold Noses and Warm Hearts was originally published as a collection of dog stories that was compiled by the late outdoor writer and humorist Corey Ford. For his 1959 edition, Ford selected pieces written by his contemporaries, many of whom were close personal friends whose names appeared alongside his on the mastheads of popular magazines such as *The New Yorker, Vanity Fair, Life, The Saturday Evening Post,* and *Collier's.* The names read like a "Who's Who" of humor: Benchley, White, Thurber, Woollcott, Wodehouse, and Marquis. Ford tossed in a smattering of stories by writers of serious fiction, too, such as Steinbeck, Lardner, Lawrence, and Kipling to equalize the mix; but by and large, his *Cold Noses* is a light-hearted look at people who are owned by their dogs.

Say, for instance, I walked along with Corey down the road apiece until we came to a fork, whereupon he took the left and I took the right. That road would be our common literary path—the dozen of the thirty stories he originally collected that I share an appreciation for, and have included in this volume. These twelve traveled exceedingly well through time. As for the remaining eighteen, if you are not in the habit of walking your poodle down Fifth Avenue, dressed in your Sunday best (you, not the poodle—the dog would be wearing a rhinestone collar) then you can understand why they didn't quite make the final cut the second time around.

The stories I bring to the new *Cold Noses and Warm*

Hearts are of a more serious bent. They focus on working dogs that are also companions and helpmates. These stories of staunch allegiance between dog and master underscore how the bond runs deep—and spans the ages. My selection includes many long-time favorites by writers such as Jim Corbett, John Hunter, Albert Payson Terhune, and Teddy Roosevelt, as well as others by lesser known authors who are new to me and became instant favorites. In an 1884 speech to the United States Senate, George Graham Vest pronounced: "The one absolutely unselfish friend that man can have in this selfish world, the one that never deserts him, the one that never proves ungrateful or treacherous, is his dog... When all other friends desert, he remains." This may be one of the rare declarations upon which that august body unanimously agreed. If you love dogs—and I think I'm safe in assuming you do—you, too, may very well agree.

—Laurie Morrow
April 1996
Freedom, New Hampshire

Parapups

By Corey Ford

Previously published in *Collier's,* Nov. 27, 1943.

Corey Ford

Corey Ford was a well-known humorist during the 1920s and 1930s, but it was really not until after World War II that he garnered his lasting reputation as an outdoor writer. During the war, however, he aspired to be nothing more or less than an enlisted soldier. Problem was, at age 39, Uncle Sam was reluctant to welcome Corey into the ranks. So, they struck a deal. Corey would come on board as a full-fledged lieutenant colonel, skipping the stepladder up the ranks, if he would agree to undertake a special assignment: chronicling the airmen's war for America.

This he did, with such enthusiasm and devotion that a nation did indeed—through magazines such as Collier's *and* Saturday Evening Post*—get a cockpit view of what it was like to fight for freedom, from literally every corner of the globe.*

Going through Corey's literary estate, however, reveals much more about the man who went to war to report on the boys. There are his diaries. And letters. Often, too often, he would write to the parents of a soldier, say eighteen, nineteen—barely a lad—who never would return home to celebrate another birthday. And they, in their grief, would reply to Corey, thanking him for watching over their boy at the end. How this affected Corey is made quite clear in his private and published wartime writings.

Always Corey would liberally spread his own brand of humor among a company of men stationed in some far-away base say, on the Aleutians, say, on Christmas Eve, or any day, for that matter. And always, in the privacy of his soul, he would carefully store his impressions and his experiences. These he then carefully crafted into stories, such as the one you are about to read. It would be a true story. It always was. That's the funny thing about Corey Ford. He never wrote anything that wasn't, in some way or in every way, based on real people and real life. Here he writes about some dogs that, in every way, were as real for the people that loved them as they're about to be for you. Sure, Corey Ford was a great outdoor writer. Fact of the matter is Ford, simply, was great.

WITH THE U.S. ARMY AIR FORCES SOMEWHERE IN ENGLAND: They're going to miss Slips at this bomber base. Slipstream is his real name, but the pilots call him Slips. It could be a tribute to his ancestors' romantic lapses in the past; for Slips is part collie, part police dog, part Scotty, and the rest G.I. floor mop. His left ear lops over and his right one sticks straight out; he has a corkscrew tail, a protruding lower lip like Mayor La Guardia's, and one brown and one yellow eye. He trots flat-footed, skidding stiffly around a corner on three legs when he races to meet an incoming plane.

Slips meets all the planes, you see. He never misses a ship that lands at the field. He was down on the line when our plane arrived, tail wagging in anticipation. One searching glance, one sniff at our uniforms; and his tail dropped, the eager light went out of his eyes, he wandered away with dull disappointment written on his absurd face. "Not very friendly?" we asked.

"It isn't that." The pilot shrugged. "He thought you might be Chad."

"Chad?"

"Went down over Hamburg last month. Slips was his dog. He still meets every plane, just in case."

Nobody remembers how Slips and Chad acquired each other. Probably it was the usual story: A rainy night, a scratch at the door of the mission hut, a whine. Or else a sergeant gunner found him outside a village pub and brought him home on the handle bars of his bicycle; or else he was slinking around the mess hall, ribs sticking out, and Chad saw him. It happens all the time. We have no idea how many stray dogs there were in England when our forces arrived here, but one thing we're sure of; they're all living at the American bases by now. Today every squadron in the Eighth Air Force owns a dog. Or, every dog owns a squadron. Owns it completely, what's more; comes and goes at will, wipes his muddy feet on any cot in the barracks, eats the prize tidbits in the packages from home, sleeps on a fleece-lined flying jacket beside the stove, is fought over and spoiled the way only an Army dog can be spoiled.

There's something about a soldier and a stray dog. They belong together. Dogs prefer a pair of khaki pants and G.I. shoes to trot beside. They obviously love parades; the first notes of assembly will bring pups scurrying from every corner of the field. The rifles, the creak of leather, the rough male outdoor life is their idea of heaven. Dogs—real dogs, that is—don't go for cushions and soft rugs and ferns; that's for cats; dogs go for rumpled blankets, and being mauled, and ordered around, and having their ears pulled or their stomachs rubbed, and sitting up with an all-night poker session waiting for the bone from a pilfered pork chop sizzling on the barracks stove at midnight. And, in turn, a soldier has something in common with a dog; maybe it's the essential homelessness of them both. When your whole personal world is a cot and a foot locker and six square feet of barracks floor, you and a dog depend on each other. That's what makes a real team: not a trotting-ahead-of-you-on-a-leash relationship, but the kind of team that shares out of the same mess kit, or marches together twenty miles on maneuvers, or coiled up on the ground and sleeps, rain or shine. (That's one thing they have in common—soldiers and dogs can sleep anywhere.) A team like Slips and Chad.

And they do everything the fliers do, these adopted pups of the Air Forces. They show up for early-morning briefings, go aloft on practice hops, even fly combat missions over enemy territory when space and an indulgent CO permits. They have proper identification disks—dog tags, of course—and standard photographs for their badges. They have their own oxygen masks to wear over their muzzles at altitudes; and when they're cold they paw at the back of a crouching tail-gunner and snuggle inside his electrically heated flying suit for warmth. They even have their own parachutes, in case they have to bail out. There's Salvo, for instance, an air-wise fox terrier with over three hundred flying hours to his credit. Salvo's a full-fledged parapup. His owner, Lt. Hugh Fletcher of Cleveland, rigged for him a specially constructed miniature chute, tested for twenty-five pounds, with a sixty-inch canopy and a static line for positive opening; and recently Salvo made a spectacularly successful test jump, landing without bruises or scratches. In fact, Lt. Fletcher says that Salvo loved it. Maintains he's the first dog to ever approach a tree from the top...

Or there's Recon, a ten-months-old Scotty owned by a waist-gunner from Texas. The gunner is a staff sergeant, and Recon has three chevrons and a single rocker clipped in the fur of his left foreleg. ("He's bucking for tech now," his owner adds.) Recon had completed five missions, and was in line for an Air Medal when he ran into trouble on his sixth raid. The Fort's engines caught fire over the Channel, and they had to ditch. The sergeant grabbed Recon under one arm, inflated his Mae West, and jumped into the drink. Recon never moved a muscle, he says; just clung patiently to his master's shoulder while he swam to the bobbing rubber dinghy, already filled with survivors. The raft was too crowded for them both; so the sergeant hoisted the pup aboard and stayed in the water himself, clinging to the rim of the raft until the Air-Sea rescue squad picked them up. The crew's having an insignia made for Recon now. It's a Scotty head in the center of a pair of silver wings.

A Hound is No Respecter of Persons

Or there is Steelwool, the dirty gray Spitz who belongs to a ground crew chief, and who defends her plane vigorously against any trespassers, including on one occasion the commanding officer of the field. At least, the crew chief says, he hasn't had a wrench or screwdriver borrowed without permission since Steelwool took over. Then there's G.I. Joe, the amiable Irish setter who is the mascot of a heavy bomber, and who astounded the entire crew, while flying on a practice mission at five thousand feet, by giving birth to a handsome litter of seven pups in an empty ammunition box.

Or Propwash—but we don't expect you to believe the story of Prop. Prop is a brown-eyed and floppy eared hound of sorts, and she belongs to a captain in the Eighth Fighter Command. Now, fighter planes are notoriously lacking in roominess, and there is no safe place to stow a pup; so Prop was trained to stay on the ground while her master was aloft. Prop obeyed implicitly; nothing could budge her from the pilot's ready room until the caption returned. Until one day, just before the squadron was due back for a sweep over France when Prop rose, to everyone's amazement, and bolted through the door and disappeared. It was a full twenty minutes later that word reached the field that a plane had crashed in a nearby wood, and the pilot had bailed out; and it was another hour before the searching parties discovered the captain sitting beside his parachute with a broken leg. But how Propwash happened to be sitting there beside him lapping his face possessively, how she had known he was in trouble and how she had found her way to his side, is something that nobody at the field can tell. Nobody but Prop.

There's no way of estimating the number of these Air Force pups. There's no way of estimating their value, for that matter. Said one C.O. whose bomber base was rapidly approaching the proportions of a dog pound: "One thing I know, I never have to worry about the boys' morale as long as I see a few dogs around." Rain, cold, missions scrubbed day after day, lack of mail, monotonous food, even losses in battle are more easily borne when there is a pup around the mission hut to fool with, and tumble over on its back, and pull its ears. A pup like Slipstream.

It's going to be a little hard to let Slips go. Somehow he's become a fixture here at the base, waiting day after day on the line as the planes land; but they know how much Slips meant to Chad. They know the letters Chad used to write to his wife back in Oklahoma City, letters that always ended with: "Slips sends his best regards" and a muddy paw-print at the bottom of the page. "Slips says he enjoyed the crackers you sent." "P.S. Would write more but Slips upset the ink." The night before that mission over Hamburg, he wrote: "Don't worry, if anything ever happens Slips will take care of you okay." So they're building a little crate now, and one of the Transport Command pilots is going to smuggle Slips across the ocean, and a couple of days later he'll be in Oklahoma City.

Fliers are inarticulate. It's hard for Chad's crew to tell Chad's wife how they feel, but they figure Slips can do it. Sometimes dogs can talk better than people.

Random Thoughts on Random Dogs

By John Steinbeck

Copyright 1955 by John Steinbeck.
Permission of McIntosh and Otis, Inc.

John Steinbeck's depiction of a struggling America torn by grief and deprivation between the two world wars won him the 1940 Pulitzer Prize for The Grapes of Wrath. *It is a Depression-era story of a poverty-stricken Oklahoma farming family's search for a better life. Basic survival was a recurrent theme for Steinbeck, and he wrote purely, deeply, and painfully of common people subjugated by uncommon circumstances. He felt the erratic pulse of Everyman, and his words broke our hearts. We wept over* Tortilla Flat *(1935),* Of Mice and Men *(1937),* East of Eden *(1952), and his final novel,* The Winter of His Discontent *(1961). He was awarded the 1962 Nobel Prize for literature.*

Steinbeck also wrote light novels, such as Cannery Row, *and screenplays, such as* Viva Zapata! *But in 1962, he penned* Travels with Charley, *the story of his cross-country journey with his beloved pet poodle—which goes to show that behind every great writer there's a dog. In "Random Thoughts of Random Dogs," Steinbeck speaks of the unbreakable tie that binds humans with canines, a bond he rates "of equal importance with the use of fire to the first man."*

Avery wise man writing recently about the emergence and development of our species suggests that the domestication of the dog was of equal importance with the use of fire to the first man. Through association with a dog, man doubled his perceptions, and besides this the dog—sleeping at dawn-man's feet— let him get a little rest undisturbed by creeping animals. The uses of the dog change. One of the first treatises on dogs in English was written by an abbess or a prioress in a great religious house. She lists the ban dog, the harrier, the dog from Spain called spaniel and used for reclaiming wounded birds, the dogs of "venerie," etc., and finally she says, "There been those smalle whyte dogges carried by ladys to draw the fleas away to theirselves." What wisdom was here. The lap dog was not a decoration but a necessity.

A dog has, in our day, changed his function. Of course, we still have hounds used for the chase and greyhounds for racing, and the pointers, setters, and spaniels for their intricate professions, but in our total dog population these are the minority. Many dogs are used as decorations but by far the greatest number are a sop for loneliness. A man's or a woman's confidant. An audience for the shy. A child to the childless. In the streets of New York between seven and nine in the morning you will see the slow procession of dog and owner proceeding from street to tree to hydrant to trashbasket. They are apartment dogs. They are taken out twice a day and, while it is a cliché, it is truly amazing how owner and dog resemble each other. They grow to walk alike, have the same set of head.

In America styles and dogs change. A few years ago the Airedale was most popular. Now it is the cocker, but the poodle is coming up. A thousand years ago I can remember when the pug was everywhere.

In America we tend to breed our non-working dogs to extremes. We breed collies with their heads so long and narrow that they can no longer find their way home. The ideal dachshund is so long and low that his spine sags. Our Dobermen are paranoid. We have developed a Boston bull with a head so large that the pups can only be born by Caesareans.

It is not wise to mourn for the apartment dog. His lifespan is nearly twice that of the country dog. His boredom is probably many times greater. One day I got in a cab and gave the address of an animal store. The driver asked, "Is it a dog you're after? Because I can let you have a dog. I got dogs!"

"It's not a dog, but how is it you have dogs?"

"It's this way," the cabby said. "It's Saturday night in an apartment and a man and his wife were lapping up a scoop of gin. About midnight they get to arguing. She says, 'Your damn dog. Who has to clean up after him and walk him and feed him, and you just come home and pat him on the head.' And the guy says, 'Don't you run down my dog.' 'I hate him,' she says. 'O.K. Pal,' he says, 'if that's the way you want it. Come on, Spot,' and he and the dog hit the street. The guy sits on a bench and holds the mutt in his arms and cries and then the two of them go to a bar and the guy tells everybody there no dame could treat his pal that way. Well, pretty soon they close the bar and it's late and the liquor begins to wear off and the guy wants to go home. So he gets in the cab and gives the dog to the cabbie. It happens to me every Saturday night."

I have owned some astonishing dogs. One I remember with pleasure was a very large English setter. He saw things unknowable. He would bark at a tree by the hour, but only at one tree. In grape season he ate nothing but grapes which he picked off the vine, one grape at a time. In pear season he subsisted on windfall pears, but he would not touch an apple. Over the years he became more and more otherworldly. I think he finally came to disbelieve in people. He thought he dreamed them. He gathered all the dogs in the neighborhood and gave them silent lectures or sermons, and one day he focused his attention on me for a full five minutes and then he walked away. I heard of him from different parts of the state. People tried to get him to stay, but in a day or so he would wander on. It is my opinion that he was a seer and that he had become a missionary. His name was T-Dog. Long later, and one hundred miles away, I saw a sign painted on a fence which said "T-God." I am convinced that he had transposed the letters of his last name and gone out into the world to carry his message to all the dogs thereof.

I have owned all kinds of dogs but there is one I have always wanted and never had. I wonder if he still exists. There used to be in the world a white English Bull Terrier. He was stocky, but quick. His muzzle was pointed and his eyes triangular so that his expression was that of cynical laughter. He was friendly and not quarrelsome, but forced into a fight, he was very good at it. He had a fine, decent sense of himself and was never craven. He was a thoughtful, inward dog, and yet he had enormous curiosity. He was heavy of bone and shoulder. Had a fine arch to his neck. His ears were sometimes cropped, but his tail never.

He was a good dog for a walk. An excellent dog to sleep beside a man's bed. He showed a delicacy of sentiment. I have always wanted one of him. I wonder whether he still exists in the world.

Dogs

By Ring Lardner

From *First and Last* by Ring Lardner.
Copyright 1934 by Charles Scribner's Sons.

His friend, F. Scott Fitzgerald said, "A noble dignity flowed from him," yet Ring Lardner looked like Buster Keaton, and his high cheekbones and gaunt face were compared with the vaulted ceiling of a cathedral. "Lardner had an ear for the dim sad music of America that nobody else could touch," said E.B. White.

Sportswriter, newspaperman, magazine columnist, and master of the short story, Lardner was a presence to be reckoned with. The formula for his stories was "cause-and-effect," as in "Bernice Bobs Her Hair," his short story about a young girl goaded by her peers into cutting her long, luxurious hair only to face their calumny.

He purposely used grammatical errors and misspellings to flesh out characters: "But if liking animals ain't a virtue in itself I don't see how it proves that a man has got any virtues." See what he means, and how he does it, in "Dogs."

Every little wile you hear people talking about a man they don't nobody seem to have much use for him on acct. of him not paying his debts or beating his wife or something, and everybody takes a rap at him about this and that until finally one of the party speaks up and says theys must be some good in him because he likes animals.

"A man can't be all bad when he is so kind to dogs." That is what they generally always say and that is the reason you see so many men stop on the st. when they see a dog and pet it because they figure that maybe somebody will looking at him do it, and the next time they are getting panned, why who ever seen it will speak up and say: "He can't be all bad because he likes dogs."

Well, friends, when you come right down to cases they's about as much sense to this as a good many other delusions that we get here in this country like for inst. the one about nobody wanting to win the first pot and the one about the whole lot of authors not being able to do their best work unless they are ½ pickled.

But if liking animals ain't a virtue in itself I don't see how it proves that a man has got any virtues, and personally, if I had a daughter and she wanted to get married and I asked her what kind of bird the guy was and she said she don't know nothing about him except that one day she seen him kiss a leopard, why I would hold up my blessing till a few of the missing precincts was heard from.

But as long as our best people has got it in their skull that a friendly feeling toward dumb brutes takes the curse off a bad egg, why I or nobody else is going to be sucker enough to come out and admit that all the horses, rams and oxens in the world could drop dead tomorrow morning without us batting an eye.

Pretty near everybody wants to be well thought of and if liking dogs or sheep is a helping along these lines, why even if I don't like them, I wouldn't never lose a opportunity to be seen in their company and act as if I was having the time of my life.

But while I was raised in a Kennel, you might say, and some of my most intimate childhood friends was of the canine gender, still in all I believe dogs is better in some climates than others, the same as oysters, and I don't think it should ought to be held against a man if he don't feel the same towards N.Y. Dogs as he felt towards Michigan dogs, and I am free to confess that the 4 dogs who I have grew to know personally here on Long Island have failed to arouse tender yearnings anyways near similar to those inspired by the flea bearers of my youth.

And in case they should be any tendency on the part of my readers to denounce me for failing to respond whole heartedly to the wiles of the Long Island breed let me present a brief sketch of some so as true lovers of the canine tribe can judge for themselfs if the fault is all mind.

No. 1

This was a dainty boy that belonged to Gene Buck and it was a bull dog no bigger than a 2 car garage and it wouldn't harm a hair of nobody's head only other animals and people. Children were as safe with this pet as walking in the Pittsburgh freight yards and he wouldn't think no more of wronging a cat than scratching himself.

In fairness to Mr. Buck I'll state that a pal of his give him the dog as a present without no comment. Well they wasn't no trouble till Gene had the dog pretty near ½ hour when they let him out. He was gone 10 minutes during which Gene received a couple of phone calls announcing more in anger than sorrow the sudden death of 2 adjacent cats of noble berth so when the dog came back Gene spanked him and give him a terrible scolding and after that he didn't kill no more cats except when he got outdoors.

But the next day De Wolf Hopper come over to call and brought his kid which the dog thought would look better with one leg and it took 5 people to get him not to operate, so after that Gene called up the Supt. of a dogs reform school and the man said he would take him and cure him of the cat habit by tying one of his victims around his neck and leaving it there for a week but he don't know how to cure the taste for young Hoppers unless De Wolf could spare the kid for a wk. after they was finished with the cat.

This proposition fell through but anyway Gene sent the dog to the reformatory and is still paying board for same.

No. 2

The people that lived three houses from the undersigned decided to move to England where it seems like you can't take dogs no more, as they asked us did we want the dog and it was very nice around children and we took it and sure enough it was O.K. in regards to children but shared this new owners feelings toward motorcycles and every time one went past the house the dog would run out and spill the contents and on Sundays when the traffic was heavy they would sometimes be as many as 4 or 5 motorcycles jehus standing on their heads in the middle of the road.

One of them finely took offense and told the dog and the justice of the peace called me up and said I would have to kill it within 24 hrs. And the only way I could think of to do the same was drown it in the bath tub and if you done that, why the bath tub wouldn't be no good no more, because it was a good sized dog and no matter how often you pulled the stopper it would still be there.

No. 3

The next door neighbors have a pro-German police dog that win a blue ribbon once but now it acts as body guard for the lady of the house and one day we was over there and the host says to slap his Mrs. on the arm and see what happened so I slapped her on the arm and I can still show you what happened.

When you dance with mine hostess this sweet little pet dances with you and watches your step and if you tred on the lady's toe he fines you a mouthful and if you and her is partners in a bridge game he lays under that table and you either bid right and play right or you get nipped.

No. 4

This is our present incumbrance which we didn't ask for him and nobody give him to us but here he is and he has got insomnia and he has picked a spot outside my window to enjoy it but not only that but he has learnt that if you jump at a screen often enough it will finally give way and the result is that they ain't a door or window on the first floor that you couldn't drive a rhinoceros through it and all the bugs that didn't already live in the house is moving in and bringing their family.

That is true record of the dogs who I have met since taking up by abode in Nassau County so when people ask me do I like dogs I say I'm crazy about them and I think they are all right in their place but it ain't Long Island.

How to Name
A Dog

By James Thurber

Copyright by James Thurber.
Permission of Harcourt Brace and Company.

A writer who sees the funny side of life when life isn't all that funny is a humorist. He absorbs, intellectualizes, and interprets the comings and goings of mankind from a slightly irregular point of view. A humorist can make us laugh, generally at ourselves, and often at our own expense. Few had the wit and wisdom to do this better than James Thurber.

Take, for example, his classic story, "The Secret Life of Walter Mitty." It is about a mild-mannered guy who daydreams of becoming a hero in the eyes of his difficult boss, domineering fiancé, and demanding mother. One day, Fate (in the form of a voluptuous blond) unexpectedly enters his life and serves him a series of circumstances that transform him into the man of the hour. He becomes everything he always wanted to be, earns the respect he coveted. Mitty gets a promotion at work, moves out of his mother's house, and marries the blond. In short, he triumphs. Triumph over daily drudgery was a recurring Thurber theme.

Whether foiled by cars that won't start, smothered by the grind at the office, or burdened with a nagging wife, a Thurber hero was convinced that he, a merely mortal man, could win over the mundane if only he persevered.

It's a tragic twist that a clear-thinking visionary such as Thurber went blind by 52. Although he lost his sight, he never lost his vision of his fellow man or, for that matter, man's best friend, as you'll discover in "How to Name a Dog."

Every few months somebody writes me and asks if I will give him a name for his dog. Several of these correspondents in the past year have wanted to know if I would mind the use of my own name for their spaniels. Spaniel owners seem to have the notion that a person could sue for invasion of privacy or defamation of character if his name were applied to a cocker without written permission, and one gentleman even insisted that we conduct our correspondence in the matter through a notary public. I have a way of letting communications of this sort fall behind my roll-top desk, but it has recently occurred to me that this is an act of evasion, if not, indeed, of plain cowardice. I have therefore decided to come straight out with the simple truth that it is as hard for me to think up a name for a dog as it is for anybody else. The idea that I am an expert in the business is probably the outcome of a piece I wrote several years ago, incautiously revealing the fact that I have owned forty or more dogs in my life. This is true, but it is also deceptive. All but five or six of my dogs were disposed of when they were puppies, and I had not gone to the trouble of giving to these impermanent residents of my house any names at all except Shut Up! and Cut That Out! and Let Go!

Names of dogs end up in 176th place in the list of things that amaze and fascinate me. Canine cognomens should be designed to impinge on the ears of dogs and not to amuse neighbors, tradespeople, and casual visitors. I remember a few dogs from the past with a faint but lingering pleasure; a farm hound named Rain, a roving Airedale named Marco Polo, a female bull terrier known as Brody because she liked to jump from moving motor cars and second-story windows, and a Peke called Darien; but that's all.

Well, there is Poker, alias *Fantome Noir,* a miniature black poodle I have come to know since I wrote the preceding paragraphs. Poker, familiarly known as Pokey, belongs to Mr. and Mrs. J.G. Gude of White Plains, and when they registered him with the American Kennel Club they decided he needed a more dignified name. It wasn't easy to explain this to their youngest child David, and his parents never did quite clear it up for him. When he was only eight, David thought the problem over for a long while and then asked his father solemnly, "If he belongs to that club, why doesn't he ever go there?" Since I wrote this piece originally, I have also heard about a sheep dog named Jupiter, which used to belong to Jimmy Cannon, journalist, critic, and man about dog shows. He reported in a recent column of his that Jupiter used to eat geraniums. I have heard of other dogs that ate flowers, but I refused to be astonished by this until I learn of one that's downed a nasturtium.

The only animals whose naming demands concentration, hard work, and ingenuity are the seeing-eye dogs. They have to be given unusual names because passers-by like to call to seeing eyers—"Here, Sport" or "Yuh, Rags" or "Don't take any wooden nickels, Rin Tin Tin." A blind man's dog with an ordinary name would continually be distracted from its work. A tyro at naming these dogs might make the mistake of picking Durocher or Teeftallow. The former is too much like Rover and the latter could easily sound like "Here, fellow" to a dog. Ten years ago I met a young man in his twenties who had been mysteriously blind for nearly five years and had been led about by a seeing-eye German shepherd during all of that time, which included several years of study at Yale. Then suddenly one night the dog's owner began to get his vision back, and within a few weeks was able to read the fine print of a telephone book. The effect on his dog was almost disastrous, and it went into a kind of nervous crack-up, since these animals are trained to the knowledge, or belief, that their owners are permanently blind. After the owner regained his vision he kept his dog, or course, not only because they had become attached to each other but because the average seeing-eye dog cannot be transferred from one person to another.

Speaking of puppies, as I was a while back, I feel that I should warn inexperienced dog owners who have discovered to their surprise and dismay a dozen puppies in a hall closet or under the floor of the barn, not to give them away. Sell them or keep them, but don't give them away. Sixty percent of persons who are given a dog for nothing bring him back sooner or later and plump him into the reluctant and unprepared lap of his former owner. The people say that they are going to Florida or can't take the dog, or that he doesn't want to go; or they point out that he eats first editions or lace curtains or spinets, or that he doesn't see eye to eye with them in the matter or housebreaking, or that he makes disparaging remarks under his breath about their friends. Anyway, they bring him back and you are stuck with him—and maybe six others. But if you charge ten or even five dollars for pups, the new owners don't dare return them. They are afraid to ask for their money back because they believe you might think they are hard up and need the five or ten dollars. Furthermore, when a mischievous puppy is returned to its former owner it invariably behaves beautifully, and the person who brought it back is likely to be regarded as an imbecile or a dog hater or both.

Names of dogs, to get back to our subject, have a range almost as wide as that of the violin. They run from such plain and simple names as Spot, Sport, Rex, Brownie to fancy appellations such as Prince Rudolph Hertenberg Gratzheim of Darndorf-Putzelhorst, and Darling Mist o' Love III of Heather Light-Holyrood—names originated by adults, all of whom in every other way, I am told, have made a normal adjustment to life. In addition to the plain and fancy categories, there are the Cynical and the Coy. Cynical names are given by people who do not like dogs too much. The most popular cynical names during the war were Mussolini, Tojo, and Adolf. I never have been able to get very far in my exploration of the minds of people who call their dogs Mussolini, Tojo, and Adolf, and I suspect the reason is that I am unable to associate with them long enough to examine what goes on in their heads. I nod, and I tell them the time of day, if they ask, and that is all. I never vote for them or ask them to have a drink. The great Coy category is perhaps the largest. The Coy people will call their pets Bubbles and Boggles and Sparkles and Twinkles and Doodles and Puffy and Lovums and Sweetums and Itsy-Bitsy and Betsy-Bye-Bye and Sugarkins. I pass these dog owners at the dogtrot, wearing a horrible fixed grin.

There is a special subdivision of the Coys that is not quite so awful, but awful enough. These people, whom we will call the Wits, own two dogs, which they name Pitter and Patter, Willy and Nilly, Helter and Skelter, Namby and Pamby, Hugger and Mugger, and even Wishy and Washy, Ups and Daisy, Fitz and Startz, Fetch and Carrie, and Pro and Connie. Then there is the Cryptic category. These people select names for some private reason and for no reason at all—except perhaps to arouse a visitor's curiosity, so that he will exclaim, "Why in the world do you call your dog that?" The Cryptic name their dogs October, Bennett's Aunt, Three Fifteen, Doc Knows, Tuesday, Home Fried, Opus 38, Ask Leslie, and Thanks for the Home Run, Emil. I make it a point simply to pat these unfortunate dogs on the head, ask no questions of their owners, and go about my business.

This article has degenerated into a piece that properly should be entitled "How Not to Name a Dog." I was afraid it would. It seems only fair to make up for this by confessing a few of the names I have given my own dogs, with the considerable help, if not, indeed, the insistence, of their mistress. Most of my dogs have been females, and they have answered, with apparent gladness, to such names as Jennie, Tessa, Julie, and Sophie. I have never owned a dog named Pamela, Jennifer, Clarissa, Jacqueline, Guinevere, or Shelmerdene.

About fifteen years ago, when I was looking for a house to buy in Connecticut, I knocked on the front door of an attractive home whose owner, my real-estate agent had told me, wanted to sell it and go back to Iowa to live. The lady agent who escorted me around had informed me that the owner of this place was a man named Strong, but a few minutes after arriving at the house, I was having a drink in the living room with Phil Stong, for it was he. We went out into the yard after a while and I saw Mr. Stong's spaniel. I called to the dog and snapped my fingers, but he seemed curiously embarrassed, like his master. "What's his name?" I asked the latter. He was cornered and there was no way out of it. "Thurber," he said, in a small frightened voice. Thurber and I shook hands, and he didn't seem to me any more depressed than any other spaniel I have met. He had, however, the expression of a bachelor on his way to a party he had tried in vain to get out of, and I think it must been this cast of countenance that had reminded Mr. Stong of the dog I draw. The dog I draw is, to be sure, much larger than a spaniel and not so shaggy, but I confess, though I am not a spaniel man, that there are certain basic resemblances between my dog and all other dogs with long ears and troubled eyes.

Perhaps I should suggest at least one name for a dog, if only to justify the title of this piece. All right, then what's the matter with Stong? It's a good name for a dog, short, firm, and effective. I recommend it to all those who have written to me for suggestions and to all those who may be at this very moment turning over in their minds the idea of asking my advice in this difficult and perplexing field of nomenclature.

Since I first set down these not too invaluable rules for naming dogs, I have heard of at least a dozen basset hounds named Thurber, a Newfoundland called Little Bears Thurber, and a bloodhound named Tiffany's Thurber. This is all right with me, so long as the owners of Thurbers do not bring them to call on me at my house in Connecticut without making arrangements in advance. Christabel, my old and imperious poodle, does not like unannounced dog visitors, and tries to get them out of the house as fast as she can. Two years ago a Hartford dog got lost in my neighborhood and finally showed up at my house. He hadn't had much, if anything, to eat for several days, and we fed him twice within three hours, to the high dismay and indignation of Christabel, who only gets one big meal a day. The wanderer was returned to its owner, through a story in the Hartford *Courant,* and quiet descended on my home until a handsome young male collie showed up one night. We had quite a time getting him out of the house. Christabel kept telling him how wonderful it was outdoors and trotting to the door, but the collie wasn't interested. I tried to pick him up, but I am too old to pick up a full-grown collie. In the end Christabel solved the problem herself by leading him outside on the promise of letting him chew one of the bones she had buried. He still keeps coming back to visit us from time to time, but Christabel has hidden her bones in new places. She will romp with the young visitor for about twenty seconds, then show her teeth and send him home. I don't do anything about the situation. After all, my home has been in charge of Christabel for a great many years now, and I never interfere with a woman's ruling a household.

The Fighting Strain

By Albert Payson Terhune

From *Buff: A Collie* by Albert Payson Terhune. Copyright 1921 by George H. Doran Company.

Many of us grew up reading Lad: A Dog, *by Albert Payson Terhune. Terhune would inspire a generation of children to beg their parents for a collie pup, and later, Hollywood and television would step in with the Lassie series. Unfortunately, we look back upon Lassie as a little too nostalgic, a little too sweet, and Terhune's Lad was affected in a backlash fashion in a similar manner. What is a pity, however, is that Terhune's capacity to understand the love between a dog and his master is unparalleled, and his stories are far from sugary. If anything, they speak quite clearly to the heart of every one of us who have, and do, love dogs. As you will see for yourself in this, the first chapter of his classic book,* Buff: A Collie.

She was a mixture of the unmixable. Not one expert in eighty could have guessed at her breed or breeds. Her coat was like a chow's, except that it was black and white and tan—as is no chow's between here and the Chinese Wall.

Her deep chest was as wide as a bulldog's; her queer little eyes slanted like a collie's; her foreface was like a Great Dane's, with its barrel muzzle and dewlaps. She was as big as a mastiff.

She was Nina, and she belonged to a well-to-do farmer named Shawe, a man who went in for registered cattle, and, as a side line, for prize collies.

To clear up, in a handful of words, the mystery of Nina's breeding, her dam was Shawe's long-pedigreed and registered and prize-winning tri-colour collie, Shawemere Queen. Her sire was Upstreet Butcherboy, the fiercest and gamest and strongest and most murderous pit-terrier ever loosed upon a doomed opponent.

Shawe had decided not to breed Shawemere Queen that season. Shawemere Queen had decided differently. Wherefore, she had broken from her enclosure by the simple method of gnawing for three hours at the rotting wood that held a rusty lock-staple.

This had chanced to befall on a night when Tug McManus had deputed the evening exercising of Upstreet Butcherboy to a new handy-man. The handy-man did not know Butcherboy's odd trick of going slack on the chain for a moment and then flinging himself forward with all his surpassing speed and still more surpassing strength.

As a result, the man came back to McManus's alone, noisily nursing three chain-torn fingers. Butcherboy trot-

ted home to his kennel at dawn, stolidly taking the whal-
ing which McManus saw fit to administer.

When Shawemere Queen's six bullet-headed pups
came into the world, sixty-three days later there was loud
and lurid blasphemy, at her master's kennels. Shawe, as
soon as he could speak with any degree of coherence, bade
his kennelman drown five of the pups at once, and to give
like treatment to the sixth as soon as its mother should
have no further need of the youngster.

At random the kennelman scooped up five-sixths of
the litter and strolled off to the horse-pond.

As a result of the monopoly the sixth puppy throve
apace. When she was eight weeks old, fate intervened
once more to save her from the horse-pond. Mrs.
Shawe's sister had come, with her two children, to spend
the summer at the farm. The children, after a glimpse of
the purebreed collie litters gambolling in the shaded
puppy-run, had clamoured loudly for a pup of their own
to play with.

Shawe knew the ways of a child with a puppy. He was
of no mind to risk chorea or rickets or fits or other ail-
ments, for any of his priceless collie babies; from such
Teddy Bear handling as the two youngsters would probably give it. Yet the clamour of the pair grew the more
plangently insistent.

Then it was that the bothered man bethought him of
the illegitimate offspring of Shawemere Queen, the nondescript pup he had planned to drown within the next
few days. The problem was solved.

Once more, peace reigned at Shawemere. And the two
children were deliriously happy in the possession of a
shaggy and shapeless morsel of puppyhood, in whose

veins coursed the ancient royal blood of pure colliedom
and the riotously battling strain of the pit-warriors.

They named their pet "Nina," after a Pomeranian they
had mauled and harassed into convulsions. And they prepared to give like treatment to their present puppy.

But a cross-breed is ever prone to be super-sturdy. The
roughly affectionate manhandling which had torn the
Pom's hair-trigger nerves and tenuous vitality to shreds had
no effect at all upon Nina. On the contrary, she waxed fat
under the dual caresses and yankings of her new owners.

Which was lucky. For, while a puppy is an ideal playmate for a child, the average child is a horrible playmate
for a puppy. With no consciousness of cruelty, children
maul or neglect or otherwise ill-treat thousands of
friendly and helpless puppies to death, every year. And
fond parents look on, with fatuous smiles, at their playful
offsprings' barbarity.

Strong and vigorous from birth, Nina began to take
on size at an amazing rate. Before she was eight months
old she stood higher at the shoulder than any collie at
Shawemere. She looked like no other dog on earth, and
she was larger by far than either of her parents.

The cleverest breeder cannot always breed his best
stock true to type. And when it comes to crossbreeding—
espeically with dogs—nothing short of Mother Nature
herself can predict the outcome.

Nina was a freak. She resembled outwardly neither
collie nor pit bull-terrier. Withal, she was not ill to look
on. There was a compact symmetry and an impression of
latent power to her. And the nondescript coat was thick
and fine. In spite of all this, she probably would have met
with a swift and reasonably merciful death on the depar-

ture of the two children, that autumn, had not Shawe realised that the youngsters had been invited to the farm for the following summer, and that the presence of their adored Nina would save some thoroughbred pup from sacrifice as a pet.

So the crossbreed was permitted to stay on, living at Shawemere on sufferance, well enough fed and housed in the stables, permitted to wander pretty much at will, but unpetted and unnoticed. The folk at the farm believed in breeding true to form. A nondescript did not interest them.

And the loss was theirs. For the gigantic young mongrel was worth cultivating. Clever, lovable, obedient, brave, she was an ideal farm dog. And wistfully she sought to win friends from among these indifferent humans. Sadly she missed the petting and the mauling of the children.

These so-called mongrels, by the way, are prone to be cleverer and stronger than any thoroughbred. Rightly trained, they are ideal chums and pets and guards—a truth too little known.

If the farm people had troubled to give Nina one-fiftieth of the attention they lavished on the kennel dogs, they would have seen to it that she did not set forth, one icy moonlight night in late November, on a restless gallop over the hills beyond the farm. And this story would not have been written.

Champion Shawemere King was one of the four greatest collies in America—perhaps on earth. He was such a dog as is bred perhaps twice in a generation—flawless in show qualities and in beauty and in mind. He had annexed the needful "fifteen points" for his championship at the first six shows to which Shawe had taken him. Everywhere, he had swept his way to "Winners" with ridiculous ease. He was the sensation of every show he went to.

Wisely, Shawe had withdrawn him from the ring while King was still in his glory. And, a few years later, the champion had been taken permanently from the kennels and had been promoted (or retired) to the rank of chief house-dog. As perfect in the home as in the ring, he was the pride and ornament of the big farmhouse.

On this particular November night of ice and moonlight, King had turned his back on the warmth of the living-room fire and the disreputable old fur rug that was his resting-place, and had stretched himself upon the veranda mat, head between forepaws; his deep-set dark eyes fixed on the highroad leading from town. Shawe had gone to town for the evening. He had forbidden King to go with him. But, collie-like, the champion had preferred waiting on the cold porch for a first glimpse of his returning master, rather than to lie in smug comfort indoors.

As he lay there he lifted his head suddenly from between his forepaws and sniffed the dead-cold air. At the same moment the patter of running feet on the icy ground caught his ear. Scent and sound came from the direction of the distant stables.

Then, athwart his gaze, loomed something big and bulky, that flashed in the white moonlight, cantering past him with an inviting backward lilt of the head as it made for the hills.

At once, on the invitation, King forgot his accruing years and his dignity. With a bound he was at Nina's side. Together the two raced madly across the yard and across the yellow road and on up into the hills.

It was a wonderful night for such a wild run. Pure-

breed and cross-breed were obsessed by the urge of it all.
Forgotten was King's stolidly loyal intent to lie on the
chilly mat until Shawe should return. Forgotten was the
wistful loneliness that had saddened Nina since the depar-
ture of the two children.

As the dogs bounded across the bright road, the
kennelman, returning from a stroll, caught sight of them
and recognised them. He shouted to King to come to heel.
The champion did not so much as look back. At Shawe's
call he would have obeyed—though with vast reluctance.
But this man was a hireling. And no dog knows better than
a collie the wide difference in the loyal obedience due to a
master and the negligible civility due to an employee. So
King kept on, at the shoulder of the galloping new mate.

When Shawe, late in January, followed the kennelman
into the corner of a disused stall and stared down at Nina,
his face was creased in a frown of disgust.

There, deep in a pile of bedding, lay the big young
crossbred dog. She looked up at the visitors with a wel-
coming glint of her round brown eyes and a thumping
wag of her bushy tail. She was happy at their notice. She
was inordinately proud of what they had come to see.

Snuggled close against her side squirmed seven puppies. They were three days old. A more motley collection
could not have been found in dogdom.

Two were short-haired and bullet-headed, and were
white except for a brindle spot or two on head and hip.
Throwbacks, these, to their warlike grandsire, Upstreet
Butcherboy. Three more were immediate of aspect, and
might or might not be going to have long coats. A sixth
was enough like a thoroughbred collie to have passed
muster in almost any newborn collie litter.

Over this harlequin sextette Shawe's contemptuous glance strayed. Then his gaze focused on the seventh pup. And the frown was merged into a look of bland incredulity.

The pup was lying an inch or two away from his dam, and several inches from the huddle of brothers and sisters. Every line of him was clearly visible and distinct from the rest.

To a layman, he looked like any three-day-old collie. To Shawe he did not. Any collie expert will tell you that at the age of three days a pup gives far truer promise of his future appearance—to the trained eye—than he gives at three months. To the man who knows, there is a look—to the head, especially—that foreshadows the lines of maturity.

Later, all this foreshadowing vanishes. At two or three months it is next to impossible to predict what the pup is going to turn into. But in that one brief phase of babyhood the future often is writ clear.

Shawe noticed the coffin-shaped skull, the square muzzle, the full foreface, the set of the tiny ears, the general conformation. Unbelieving, he stared. He picked up the wiggling morsel of fur and flesh and looked more closely at those prophetic head-lines.

"Good Lord!" he mumbled, bewildered, "why-why, that's a-a DOG! He's the living image of what King was, at three days. And I picked out King for a great collie when he was this youngster's age. I've never known it to fail. Never, up to now. What's this measly mongrel doing with the head and build of a winner?"

"Well," ruminated the kennelman, "we know he's three-quarter bred, don't we?" King's his sire. And Shawemere Queen was his dam's mother. Best blood anywhere in colliedom, ain't it? And it had to come out, somewheres, didn't it? Cross-breeding ain't like mixing feed. You don't get the same mixture, every measureful you dip out. Some is all one kind and some is all another, and some ain't neither. Look at them two white fellows! They're straight bull-pup. (Wherever they got it!) Not a trace of collie to 'em. It's got be av'raged up, somewheres. And it's av'raged up in that little cuss you're holding there. He's all collie. Just like the two whitish ones is all bull. It's…"

"I've—I've heard of such cases," muttered Shawe wonderingly, as he laid the tiny pup back at the mother's side. "But—oh, he'll most likely develop a body that'll give him away! Or else the head won't live up to its promise. Well, leave him, anyhow, when you drown the rest. That can't do any harm."

Sheepishly, he gave the order. Still more sheepishly, as he left the stall, he stooped and patted Nina's lovingly upraised head—the first caress he had ever wasted on the lonely cross-breed.

Thus it was that a great dog was born; and that his promise of greatness was discovered barely in time to save him from death in earliest babyhood. For the collie—or near-collie—pup was destined to greatness, both of body and of brain.

Shawe named him "Buff." This, of course, without the honorary prefix of the kennel name, "Shawemere." For Buff could never be registered. His spotty pedigree could never be certified. He could claim no line in the American Kennel Club's Studbook. He was without recognised lineage; without the right to wear a number after his name.

A dog, to be registered, must come of registered parents. These parents, in turn, must come of registered stock; since no dog, ordinarily, is eligible to registration unless both his sire and dam have been registered. That means his race must have been pure and his blood of unmingled azure since the beginning of his breed's recognition by the studbooks.

Buff's sire could have traced his genealogy back, in an unbroken line, for centuries. King's nearer ancestors had been the peerless noblemen of dogdom. Nina's sire and dam—though of widely different stock—were born to the purple. Despite all this, their descendant was a mongrel and barred by Kennel law from any bench show.

The nameless pup grew to beautiful doghood. To all outward appearance, he was a pure-bred collie of the very highest type. The head was classic in its perfection. The body had the long, wolf-like lines of the true collie. The coat was a marvel. The chest was deep and broad, the body powerfully graceful. No collie judge, unhung, could have detected the bar-sinister.

The mind and the soul and the heart, too, were of the true collie sort. But, blended with the fiery gaiety and dash of his predominant breed, ran unseen the steadfastness, the calm, the grimness, the stark warrior spirit of the pit-bull terrier.

This same strain ran, equally unseen, through the physique as well; giving un-collielike staunchness and iron strength and endurance to the graceful frame; imparting an added depth of chest, a gripping and rending quality to the jaw muscles; a mystic battling genius to body and to spirit.

Yes, old Upstreet Butcherboy was present in this collie grandson of his. So were a hundred mighty bull-terrier ancestors. It was a strange blend. Yet it was a blend; not a mixture. Nature, for once, had been kind, and had sought

to atone for the cruel joke she had played in the making
of poor, neglected Nina.

The first half year or more of Buff's life passed pleas-
antly enough at Shawemere. At the age of three months
he was moved from the stables and put in one of the
puppy runs. Nina was miserable at her baby's abduction.
Whenever she was loose she would rush up to the puppy-
runs and canter whimperingly around their wire bound-
aries, seeking to attract her little son's attention.

And always, at first sight or sound or scent of her, Buff
would leave his fellow pups and come hurrying to the wire
to greet her. Through the wide meshes their noses would
meet in a sniffing kiss; and with wagging tails they would
stand in apparent converse for minutes at a time. It was a
pretty sight, this greeting and talk between the young aris-
tocrat and his mongrel mother. But, at Shawemere, dogs
were bred for points and for sale; not for sentiment.

At first, Buff was wretchedly lonely for Nina. In the
daytime it was not so bad. For there was much to amuse
and excite him in the populous puppy-run. But at night,
when the rest were asleep, he missed his mother's warm
fur and her loving companionship. To some extent, this
homesickness for her wore off. But never entirely. Always
Buff sought means to get back to her. And their frequent
meetings, on opposite sides of the wire meshes, kept the
impulse alive in his heart.

The run contained a nine-pup litter, a couple of
months older than little Buff. The biggest pup of the litter, on the hour of Buff's arrival, undertook to teach the
lonesome baby his place. This he did by falling unexpectedly upon Buff as the latter stood disconsolately at the
fence looking for his absent mother. The bully attacked

the small newcomer with much bluster and growling and show of youthful ferocity.

It was Buff's first encounter with an enemy—his first hint that the world was not made up wholly of friendliness. And it staggered him. Making no resistance at all, he crouched humbly under the fierce attack. The bully, at this sign of humility, proceeded to follow up his advantage by digging his milk teeth into Buff's soft ear.

The bite stung, and with the sting came a swirl of wholesome indignation into the exiled baby's hitherto peace-loving brain. Away back in his cosmos snarled the spirit of Upstreet Butcherboy. Scarce knowing what he did, he flashed from under the larger body and made a lightning lunge for the bully's throat.

Subconscious fighting skill guided the counter-assault and lent zest to the grappling youngster's onset. As a result, some five seconds later, the bully was on his back, squalling right piteously for mercy from the opponent that was barely two-thirds his size, and half his age.

By this time, Buff had shifted his vise-like grip from throat to forelegs, and thence to stomach. For, along with the pit terrier's instinct for biting hard and holding on, he had inherited his collie forbears' knack of being everywhere at once in a fight; and of changing one hold for a better at an instant's notice. Which unusual combination would have delighted the soul of any professional dogfighter.

Yet, the moment the bully was cowed into subjection, Buff let him up. Nor did he—at food trough or elsewhere—seek to take advantage of his new position as boss of the run. He did not care to harass and terrorize lesser pups. He preferred to be friends with all the world, as he had been with his dear and friendly mother.

And so time wore on—time that shaped the roly-poly Buff into a leggy but handsome six-months' pup. And now the promise of the three-day baby was fulfilled, more and more every hour. With puzzled pride Shawe used to stand and inspect him. The pup was shaping into a true winner. But what could be done with him—minus pedigree and plus bar-sinister as he was? If Buff had been a thoroughbred he would have been worth a small fortune to his owner. But now—

Again fate settled the problem—once and for all.

It was the night after the kennelman had put collars for the first time on all the pups in Buff's yard. These collars were of a rudimentary sort, and for use only long enough to accustom the young necks to such burden. Each collar was a circle of clothesline, with buckle and tongue attached, and with its wearer's "kennel name"—a very different title from the lofty "pedigree name"—scribbled on a tag attached to the steel tongue.

Buff did not like his collar at all. It fidgeted him and made him nervous. The name-tage flapped tantalisingly just beneath the reach of his jaws; which added to the annoyance. That was one reason why Buff could not sleep. After a time he gave up the effort at slumber, and came out of the sleeping quarters where his companions were snoozing in furry comfort.

He made a few futile attempts to get the fluttering tag between his teeth and to rub off the collar against the wire meshes. Then, with a sign of annoyance, he stretched himself out on the ground near the yard's gate.

He was still lying there when the kennelman came to fill the yard's water-pans before going to bed. As all the pups, presumably, were asleep in their houses, the man did not bother to shut the wire gate behind him as he entered the yard.

Buff saw the open portal. Beyond, somewhere in the dense darkness, were the stables where his mother lived. His mother had always been able to solve his few perplexities and soothe his hurts in the days when he still had lived with her. Doubtless she could help him worry off this miserable collar and tag.

On the instant, the pup trotted out, through the swinging gate, without so much as a glance at the dimly seen man who was bending over the row of pans. And in another second the truant was in the road, sniffing to locate the stables.

But the wind set strong from the opposite direction that night. It brought Buff a faint whiff of stables, it is true; but they were the stables of a farm a mile down the turnpike.

Now, though stable scents have been Buff's earliest memory, yet he did not know there were any other stables extant besides those in which he had been born. So, locating the odour, he ambled eagerly off down the road in search of his mother.

Perhaps the length of the journey puzzled him, but, as every step brought the scent stronger, he kept on. At a bend in the road, a half-mile below, he struck off into the fields and woods, taking the shortest cut to the source of the ever-increasing odour.

A furlong from the road, his way led through a thick copse. Into it he galloped merrily. In its exact centre his run was halted with much abruptness. Something touched him on the chest, and in the same instant, tightened painfully about his neck.

Buff snorted with scared anger and lunged forward. The thing about his neck promptly cut off his breathing apparatus, and dug deep into his soft flesh. Resisting the panic impulse, Buff ceased to plunge and roll, and sought to find out what had caught him.

He had run full into the middle of one of several nooses, cunningly strung through the copse, for foxes.

Twisting his head, he seized the noose's taut end between his jaws and fell to gnawing. But he had his labour for his pains. The thin rope was braided with strands of copper wire, against just such a move on the part of some fox.

At gray dawn, the hired man of the farm, toward which Buff had been faring, came out to look at his traps. All the nooses but one hung limp. In one writhed and struggled a very tired little collie. At sight of the farmhand, Buff stopped struggling and wagged his tail. All humans, so far as he knew, were friendly to dogs. Here, presumably, was a rescuer. And Buff greeted him with warm cordiality.

The man stood gaping at him for a space. Then a slow grin began to crease his leathery mouth. This was no fox he had caught. But it was something that might well prove as valuable. He knew Shawemere, and had often seen the Shawemere collies. He had heard that the Shawemere pups brought big prices. Here, evidently, was one of those pups—a Shawemere collie that had strayed in the night and had been noosed. By taking the dog back to its home he might, perhaps, annex a five-dollar reward; but scarcely more. There seemed better ways of capitalising his treasure trove. Paying no heed to Buff's friendly advances the man left him there, hurried home, received grudging permission for a half-day off, to visit the dentist in town, and presently returned to the copse, with a pig-crate over his shoulder.

It was market-day at the near-by town. And this would not be the first or the tenth time a dog had been exhibited for sale in the market enclosure. So, a hundred yards from his destination, the man lifted the pup from the too-tight crate and fastened a rope to his collar. Then he prepared to lead his prize across to the market.

But a dog that has never before been led has to be trained to follow at the gentle tug of the leash. This training sometimes takes only a few minutes, it is true. But it is needful. Now, never before had Buff been on the end of a leash. He did not know what to do. He had lost, moreover, his early liking for his captor, and he wanted to go home.

At first tug of the rope the puppy braced all four feet, and pulled back. A tired-looking man, passing, in a still more tired looking motor run-about, slowed his car at sight of the puppy's resistance, and scanned Buff appraisingly. A second and more vehement yank of the rope, accompanied by a mouthful of profanity from the hired man, brought renewed resistance from Buff, and brought the stranger's slowing car to a complete stop.

Buff braced his feet and sought in vain to get some sort of purchase for his claws on the stone pavement. His conductor gave the rope a vicious jerk and struck the puppy over the side of the head.

This was the first blow received by Buff in all his short life. He did not at all grasp its meaning. But it hurt like the mischief, and it set his delicate ears to ringing. Incidentally, it brought the stranger, at one jump, out of his car and on to the narrow pathway.

"You idiot!" exhorted he, striding up to the farm-hand. "Don't you know any better than to hit a collie over the head? It might—"

"Don't you know no better'n to butt in?" retorted the wrathful hired man. "I'll make this mangy cuss mind me, if I have to bust ev'ry bone in his wuthless carcass!"

By way of emphasising his intention, he lifted the amazed Buff clean off the ground on the end of the rope, and drew back one large-booted foot for a drop-kick at the swinging youngster that had dared to disobey him. The kick might well have smashed every rib in the soft young body, besides rupturing its victim. But it did not reach its mark.

The tired-looking man did two things, and he did them in practically the same gesture. With his left hand he jerked the rope from the calloused hand that held it, and lowered Buff gently to earth. With his right he caught the farmhand deftly by the nape of his neck, spun him around, and bestowed upon him two swift but effective kicks.

Both kicks smote the amazed labourer approximately at the point where his short jacket's hem met the seat of his trousers. As his assailant at the same time released his hold of the shirt collar, his victim collapsed in a blasphemous heap at the gutter edge.

Buff had been watching the brief exhibition with keen interest. Gradually it had been dawning on his unsophisticated mind that his escort was trying in some way to harm him, and that the stranger had not only averted the harm, but was punishing the aggressor.

So, in his babyhood, had Nina flown at a stable cat which had scratched Buff's too-inquisitive nose. Once more the puppy knew the glad thrill of having a protector.

As the fallen man scrambled to his feet, the stranger felt a cold and grateful little nose thrust into his palm. Instinctively—and with unconscious proprietorship—his hand dropped lightly on the silken head of the dog. But he kept his tired eyes unwaveringly on the man whom he had assaulted.

The latter was on his feet again, swearing and gesticulating. But, all at once, in the middle of a contemplated rush at his antagonist, he checked himself and looked worriedly up and down the deserted lane. In case of interference—in case of court proceedings—he might have trouble in explaining his possession of the dog. A dozen persons in court might well recognize the puppy as belonging to Shawemere. And there would be difficulties—all manner of difficulties—perhaps a jail term. Decidedly it was a moment for wile, rather than for force. There were worse things than a kick. Jail was one of them.

"If you're so stuck on the pup, why don't you buy him?" he whined. "Stead of pickin' on a poor man what's got a livin' to earn? He's for sale."

"I'm not buying livestock..." began the stranger.

Then he paused. The silken head under his hand shifted, and the cold little nose again nuzzled his palm.

"If you ain't buyin'," retorted the farm-hand, "give him back to me, and I'll take him to where I c'n git an offer on him."

He snatched the rope before the tired-looking man was aware of the intention. But Buff was aware of it—well aware of it. As the rough fingers grabbed at his collar, the youngster growled fiercely and launched himself at the tyrant.

"Good!" applauded the stranger, catching the angry puppy in mid-air and holding him under one arm. "He's got pluck! That means you haven't had him long. If you had, you'd have cowed or killed him, or made him mean and savage. He's thoroughbred, too. What do you want for him? If the price is fair, I'll buy. If it isn't, I'll carry him to the nearest police-station. Which is it to be?"

Our of a volley of indignant denial, punctuated by such stock phrases as, "I'm an honest man!" and the like, came at last the grunted words.

"Thutty dollars. He's wuth a sight more. But he b'longs to my boy, and we're movin', so I gotta sell him, an'…"

"Here's the cash," interrupted the stranger, taking out some greasy notes. "But, next time you steal a dog of this kind, just remember that thirty dollars is a fool's offer. It proves the dog is stolen. There's no use asking whom you stole him from. If there were, I might be able to return him. I had no idea of cluttering my life with anything again—even with a dog. But if I don't you'll maltreat him. And he's too good for that. There are easier ways, you know, of showing how much inferior you are to a dog, than by kicking him."

The stranger was doling out bill after bill from his thin roll. Finishing, he stuck to rest of his money back into his pocket, picked up Buff, and started for his car. Midway, he hesitated; and looked back at the gaping and muttering farm-hand.

"By the way," he said carelessly, "think twice before you steal again. Not for the sake of your alleged soul, but because it's liable to land you in a cell. Nothing is valuable enough to steal. A cell isn't a pleasant place to live in, either. I know," he added as an afterthought, "because I've just come out of one."

He lifted Buff into the car, cranked the muddy and

battered little vehicle, and climbed aboard. Then, as the farm-hand still gaped at him with a new respect in the bulgingly bloodshot eyes, the stranger called back:

"If you decide to tell this dog's owner what has become of him, my name is Trent—Michael Trent. And I live at Boone Lake, about fifty miles south of here. At least, I used to—and I'm on my way back there."

It was Buff's first ride. For a few minutes it startled him to see the countryside running backwards on either side of him, and to feel the bumping vibration and throb of the car under his feet. But almost at once he felt the joy of the new sensation, as does the average dog that gets a chance to motor.

Besides, this rescuer of his was a most interesting person, a man whose latent strength appealed to Buff's canine hero-worship; a man, too, who was unhappy. And, with true collie perception, Buff realized and warmed to the human's unhappiness.

Added to all this, Trent had a delightful way of taking one hand from the steering-wheel from time to time and patting or rumpling the puppy's head. Once the strong slender fingers found the name tag.

" 'Buff,' hey!" murmured Trent. "Is that your name or the colour of the goods that were marked by this tag? How about it, Buff?"

He accented the last word. In response, Buff's tail began to wag, and one forepaw went up to the man's knee.

" 'Buff' it is," nodded Trent. "And a good little name at that. A good little name for a good little dog. And now that I've gone broke, in buying you, will you please tell what I'm going to do with you? I'm an outcast, you know, Buff. An Ishmaelite. And I'm on my way back to my home-place to live things down. It'll be a tough job, Buff. All kinds of rotten times ahead. Want to face it with me?"

Much did Trent talk to the dog during that long and bumpy drive. His voice was pleasant, to his little chum. And it was the first time in Buff's six months of life that a human had troubled to waste three sentences of speech on him. The attention tickled the lonely pup. His heart was warming more and more to this tired-eyed, quiet-voiced new master of his.

Closer he cuddled to the man's knee, looking up into the prison-pale face with growing eagerness and interest. There was a wistfulness in Buff's deep-set eyes as he gazed. With tense effort he was trying to grasp the meaning of the unknown words wherewith from time to time Trent favoured him. The man noted the pathetic eagerness of look, and his own desolate heart warmed to this first interested listener he had encountered in more than a year. He expanded under the flattening attention, and his talk waxed less disjointed.

"Yes," he said presently, stroking the puppy's head as it rested against his knee, "we've a tough row to hoe, you and I, Buff. Just as I told you. Since you're so different from two-footed curs, that you're willing to associate with a jail-bird, perhaps it'd amuse you to hear how I came to be one. Eh, Buff?"

At each repetition of his name, Buff wagged his tail in delight at hearing at least one word whose meaning he knew.

"Not to take up too much of your time, Buff," proceeded Trent, trying to negotiate a rutted bit of road with one hand while with the other he sought to ease the bumping of the car for the dog, "here's the main idea: I'd just got that farm of mine on a paying basis, and changed it from a liability to something like an asset, when the smash-up came. Just because I chose to play the fool. It was down at the Boone Lake store one night. I had walked into town for the mail. It was being sorted. And on the mail stage had come two biggish boxes of goods for Corney Fales. He's the storekeeper and postmaster there, Buff."

Again, at his name, Buff wagged his tail and thrust his cold nose into Trent's free hand.

"The boxes were left on the store porch while Fales sorted the mail," went on Trent. "It struck me it would be a corking joke to carry them out behind a clump of lilacs to one side of the store, where it was black dark that night. I hid them there for the fun of hearing old Fales swear when he found them gone. Well, he swore, good and plenty. And by the time he'd sworn himself out, I'd had about enough of the joke. And I was just going to tell him about it and help him carry the boxes back to the store, when a couple of chaps—that I'd ordered off my land the week before—stepped up and told him they'd seen me lug the boxes away in the dark. So I went out to the lilac clump to get the stuff and carry it back to Fales.

"And, Buff, the boxes weren't there. They'd been stolen in dead earnest while I had been standing in the store laughing at Fales's red-hot language. It had been a silly joke, at best, for a grown man to play, Buff.

"And, anyhow, nobody but a born fool ever plays practical jokes. Always remember that, Buff. But you know how a fellow will limber up sometimes after a lonely day's work, and how he'll do silly things. Well, that's how it happened, Buff.

"Of course I owned up, and offered to pay the sixty dollars Fales said the goods were worth. But he wouldn't have it that way. It seemed he'd been missing things for quite a while. And his pig-headed brain got full of the idea I had taken them all, and that I'd pretended it was a joke when I was caught at last. So he prosecuted. And the county attorney was looking for a record. And he got it, Buff. He sure got it.

"I was sent up for eighteen months. Just for being a fool. And perhaps I'm a fool to go back now and pick up life again in a place where everyone thinks I'm a thief. But that's what I'm going to do, Buff. I'm going to win through. It'll take a heap of time and a heap more nerve to do it. But—well, we're headed for Boone Lake. The sooner we begin the fight the sooner we'll win it."

He paused, half ashamed of his babbling, yet half relieved at being able to speak out at last to some listener who did not greet the tale with a grin of incredulity. Buff snuggled the closer to him, and licked his clenched hand as the pain underlying the light speech struck upon the collie's sensitive perceptions.

"Good little pal!" approved Trent, touched at the wordless sympathy and feeling somehow less desolate and miserable than he had felt for many a long month.

It was mid-afternoon when they drove through the edge of a rambling village and on for a mile or so to a lane that led into a neglected farm.

"This is home, Buff!" announced Trent, his eyes dwelling with sharp unhappiness upon the tumbledown aspect of the deserted place. "Home—including the mortgage that went on it to pay for my lawyer. Did you notice how those village people stared at us, and how they nudged each other? Well, that's just the first dose. A sort of sample package. Are you game to stand for the rest of it? I am, if you are."

Running the battered car into a shed, Trent lifted Buff to the ground and set off towards the closed and forbidding house. Buff capered on ahead of him, trotting back at every ten paces to make sure his master was following.

Trent paused for a moment in the dooryard to grope in his pocket for a key. Buff had gained the summit of the low veranda. As Trent halted the pup took advantage of the delay to rest his car-cramped muscles by stretching out at full length on the narrow strip of porch. Trent took a step forward, then stopped again; this time to stare in bewildered surprise at the collie. For he noted that Buff was lying like a couchant lion, so far as his forequarters were concerned, but that his hind-legs were both stretched out straight behind him.

Now, as Trent's dog-lore told him, that is a position in which no collie lies. Nor does any dog lie with his hind legs out behind him, unless he has in his make-up a strong admixture of bull-dog blood. Yes, Trent's dog-knowledge also told him that this was apparently a pure-bred collie; perfect in every point. Wherefore, he stared in wonder at the phenomenon of Buff's position.

Then, giving up the problem, he advanced into the house. Buff, springing up at once, followed Trent inquisitively through the doorway, as the key turned noiselessly in the lock and the front door swung open under the pressure of the man's knee. Out gushed the musty odour that haunts unused country houses. It filled Trent's nostrils and deepened his sense of desolation. But, mingled with the smell of emptiness and disuse, another and more definite scent assailed Trent's nose. It was the reek of tobacco—of rank pipe tobacco, at that. Nor was it stale.

At the whiff of it Trent stiffened like a pointing dog. His lips had been parted in a careless word to Buff. Now he choked back the unborn syllables.

Treading on tiptoe, he made his way from room to room. Buff, sensing the other's efforts at silence, padded quietly at his heels. As they moved along, Trent paused from time to time, to sniff the heavy air.

Presently he flung open a door, with no caution whatever, and sprang into a room beyond. It was the kitchen he entered in this whirlwind fashion. And he saw, as his nose had told him, that it was already occupied. A mattress had been hauled hither from one of the bedrooms. Sprawled thereon were two men. One of these was snoring, the other was puffing a clay pipe.

On the floor beside them lay a full sack. Piled in a corner of the room was a heterogeneous stack of household articles—a clock, a silver candlestick, three gilt picture-frames, a plated soup-tureen, some spoons, and similar loot. Trent had scarce time to note these facts and a heap of empty bottles in another corner, before the smoker had dropped his pipe with a grunt and sprung scramblingly to his feet. The sleeping man, roused by his companion's noise, sat up and blinked.

"H'm!" mused Trent, as the two stared owlishly at him. "I see. You boys didn't reckon on my time off for good behavior, eh? Thought I wasn't due home for another month or so; and in the meantime this was a dandy place to hide in and to keep the stuff you steal? Clever lads! H'm!"

The two still blinked dully at him. Evidently their density was intensified by the contents of some of the empty bottles lying near the mattress.

"I'm beginning to understand things," pursued Trent evenly. "You two testified you saw me take away those boxes from Fales' store. I went to prison on your testimony. You had lived hereabouts all your lives, and there was nothing known against either of you. So your word was good enough to send me up—while you pinched the boxes, and plenty of other things. Since then"—with a glance at the plunder—"you seem to have gone into the business pretty extensively. And you picked the safest place to keep it in. Now, suppose you both…"

He got no further. By tacit consent, the two lurched to their feet and flung themselves upon him.

But, careless as had been his pose and his tone, Trent had not been napping. Even as he spoke, he realized what a stroke of cleverness it would be for the men to overpower him and to claim that they had found him in his own house surrounded by these stolen goods. It would be so easy a way to fix the blame of such recent robberies as had scourged Boone Lake on some unknown accomplice of Trent's! The craft that had once made them take advantage of his joke on Fales would readily serve them again.

But as they flung themselves on Trent, he was no longer there. In fact, he was nowhere in particular. Also he was everywhere. Agile as a lynx, he was springing aside from their clumsy rush, then dashing in and striking with all his whalebone strength; dodging, blocking, eluding, attacking; all in the same dazzlingly swift set of motions. It was a pretty sight.

A prolonged carouse on raw whiskey is not the best training for body or for mind in an impromptu fight. And the two trespassers speedily discovered this. Their man was all over them, yet ever out of reach. Too stupidly besotted to use teamwork, they impeded rather than reinforced each other. Up and down the broad kitchen raged the trio.

Then, ducking a wild swing, Trent darted in and uppercut one of his antagonists. The man's own momentum, in the swing, added fifty per cent to the impetus of Trent's blow. Trent's left fist caught his enemy flush on the jaw-point. The man's knees turned to tallow. He slumped to the floor in a huddled heap.

Not so much as waiting to note the effect of his uppercut. Trent was at the other thief; rushing him off his feet and across the room with a lightning series of short-arm blows that crashed through the awkward defense and landed thuddingly on heart and wind. In another few seconds the fight must have ended—and ended with a second clean knock-out—had not one of Trent's dancing toes chanced to light on a smear of bacon fat on the smooth floor.

Up went both of his feet. He struck ground on the back of his head, after the manner of a novice skater. And, half stunned, he strove to rise. But the impact had, for the moment, knocked the speed and the vigor out of him. Before he could stagger half-way to his feet his opponent had taken dizzy advantage of the slip. Snatching up one of the big bottles by the neck, the thief swung it aloft, measuring with his eye the distance and force needful to a blow over the head of the reeling and dazed Trent.

Then the blow fell. But it did not fall upon Trent. It missed him by an inch or more, and the bottle smashed

into many pieces on the boards. This through no awk-
wardness of the assailant, but because a new warrior had
entered the fray.

A flash of gold and white spun through the air, as the
bottle was brandished aloft; and a double set of white
teeth buried themselves in the striking arm.

Buff, from the doorway, had been watching the battle
with quivering excitement. In his brief life he had never
before seen prolonged strife among humans. And he did
not understand it. To him it seemed these men must be
romping, as he and the other inmates of the puppy run
had been wont to romp. And he watched the wild performance in breathless interest.

But, all at once, his master was down. And, above
him, his foe was brandishing something. Thus menac-
ingly had been raised from the farm-hand's arm when
Buff was struck. Surely this was not a romp! His master
was threatened. And into the fight gallant young Buff
hurled himself—attacking the arm that menaced the
quiet-voiced man he was learning to adore.

Just below the elbow he found his grip. Deep drove
the sharp white teeth; not slashing, collie fashion, but
with the grim holding power that had won a score of bat-
tles for old Upstreet Butcherboy. On the swung canvas
strip, a hundred of his bull terrier ancestors had been
made to strengthen the crushingly powerful jaw muscles
they had bequeathed to Buff.

The pup's forty pounds of squirming weight
deflected the blow's aim, and saved Trent's skull from
certain fracture.

The thief, in pain and terror, tore at the clinging furry
body in frantic rage. But the bulldog jaws were locked,

and the fearless collie spirit refused to unlock them at the yells and the hammerings of the panic-stricken thief.

All this for the merest second. Then, still dizzy, but himself again, Trent was up and at his foe.

The rest was conquest.

Hampered by the ferocious beast that clung to his right arm—weak from pain and exertion—the man was ridiculously easy to overcome.

"You've won your welcome, Buff, old chum!" panted Trent, as he trussed up his prisoners, before marching them to the village. "And you've saved a life I don't value overmuch. But you've done a lot more. You've let me clear myself of the other charge. These men will have to talk when the police sweat them. And that will make life worth while for me again. Yes, you've paid your way, all right! Something tells me you and I are going to be the best pals ever. But—where in blue blazes did a thorough-bred collie ever pick up that bulldog grip?"

The Care and Training of a Dog

By E.B. White

From *One Man's Meat* by E.B. White.
Copyright 1940 by E.B. White.
Permission of Harper & Brothers.

E.B. White is popularly associated with an adorable pig, a loving spider, and a bunch of farm animals. He wrote Charlotte's Web *in 1952, and like other children's classics such as* Peter Pan, The Secret Garden, Black Beauty, The Wind in the Willows, *it too weaves endless magic that never frays for young and old alike.*

E.B. White was acclaimed as America's greatest paragraphist, or writer of essays. Clever, conversational, easygoing, White's "Notes and Comments" columns in The New Yorker *were so popular they became known as "White casuals." He defined humor as "a sly and almost imperceptible ingredient that sometimes gets into writing." The ingredients in his recipe for veiled humor were a dash of wit, a pinch of whimsy, and a shake of satire, parody, and pun stirred into one essay.*

Satirist Marc Connelly claimed he "brought steel and fire" to his columns. Humorist Corey Ford labeled White's essays "poetry-in-prose." Yet the country's greatest stylist was a painfully shy, introspective man. Ford first met him at The New Yorker. *He shook White's hand, saying how much he enjoyed his column. Abruptly, White left the room. Taken aback, Ford looked over at the editor-in-chief Harold Ross for an explanation. "You sca-a-ared him!" Ross snarled.*

White's simple, bittersweet sentiment in "The Care and Training of a Dog" speaks volumes. Of his favorite canine companion, Write writes: "When I got him he was what I badly needed." A lot of us know what he means.

The possession of a dog today is a different thing from the possession of a dog at the turn of the century, when one's dog was fed on mashed potato and brown gravy and lived in a doghouse with an arched portal. Today a dog is fed on scraped beef and Vitamin B1, and lives in bed with you.

An awful lot of nonsense has been written about dogs by persons who don't know them very well, and the attempt to elevate the pure-bred to a position of national elegance has been, in the main, a success. Dogs used to mate with other dogs rather casually in my day, and the results were discouraging to the American Kennel Club but entirely satisfactory to small boys who liked puppies. In my suburban town, "respectable" people didn't keep she-dogs. One's washerwoman might keep a bitch, or one's lawn cutter, but not one's next-door neighbor.

The prejudice against females made a great impression on me, and I grew up thinking that there was something indecent and unclean about she-things in general. The word bitch of course was never used in polite families. One day a little mutt followed me home from school, and after much talk I persuaded my parents to let me keep it—or at least until the owner turned up or advertised for it. It dwelt among us only one night. Next morning my father took me aside and in a low voice said: "My son, I don't know whether you realize it, but that dog is a female. It'll have to go."

"But why does it have to?" I asked.

"They're a nuisance," he replied, embarrassed. "We'd have all the other dogs in the neighborhood around here all the time."

That sounded like an idyllic arrangement to me, but I

could tell from my father's voice that the stray dog was doomed. We turned her out and she went off toward the more liberal section of town.

On our block, in the days of my innocence, there were in addition to my collie, a pug dog, a dachshund named Bruno, a fox terrier named Sunny who spent many years studying one croquet ball, a red setter, and a St. Bernard who carried his mistress's handbag, snuffling along in stately fashion with the drool running out both sides of his jaws. I was scared of this St. Bernard because of his size, and never passed his house without dread. The dachshund was old, surly, and disagreeable, and was endlessly burying bones in the flower border of the De Vries's yard. I should very much doubt if any of those animals ever had its temperature taken rectally, ever was fed raw meat or tomato juice, ever was given distemper inoculations, or ever saw the whites of a veterinary's eyes. They were brought up on chicken bones and gravy and left-over cereal, and were all fine dogs. Most of them never saw the inside of their houses—they knew their place.

The "problem" of caring for a dog has been unnecessarily complicated. Take the matter of housebreaking. In the suburbia of those lovely post-Victorian days of which I write the question of housebreaking a puppy was met with the simple bold courage characteristic of our forefathers. You simply kept the house away from the puppy. This was not only the simplest way, it was the only practical way, just as it is today. Our parents were in possession of a vital secret—a secret which has been all but lost to the world: the knowledge that a puppy will live and thrive without ever crossing the threshold of a dwelling house, at least till he's big enough so he doesn't wet the rug.

Although our fathers and mothers very sensibly never permitted a puppy to come into the house, they made up for this indignity by always calling the puppy "Sir." In those days a dog didn't expect anything very elaborate in the way of food or medical care, but he did expect to be addressed civilly.

A really companionable and indispensable dog is an accident of nature. You can't get it by breeding for it, and you can't buy it with money. It just happens along. Out of the vast sea of assorted dogs that I have had dealings with, by far the noblest, the best, and the most important was the first, the one my sister sent me in a crate. He was an old-style collie, beautifully marked, with a blunt nose, and great natural gentleness and intelligence. When I got him he was what I badly needed. I think probably all these other dogs of mine have been just a groping toward that old dream. I've never dared get another collie for fear the comparison would be too uncomfortable. I can still see my first dog in all the moods and situations that memory has filed him away in, but I think of him oftenest as he used to be right after breakfast on the back porch, listlessly eating up a dish of petrified oatmeal rather than hurt my feelings. For six years he met me at the same place after school and convoyed me home—a service he thought up himself. A boy doesn't forget that sort of association.

Robin

By Jim Corbett

From *Man-eaters of Kumaon.*
Copyright 1946 by Oxford University Press.

I never saw either of his parents. The Knight of the Broom I purchased him from said he was a spaniel, that his name was Pincha, and that his father was a "Keen gun dog." This is all I can tell you about his pedigree.

I did not want a pup, and it was quite by accident that I happened to be with a friend when the litter of seven was decanted from a very filthy basket for her inspection. Pincha was the smallest and the thinnest of the litter, and it was quite evident he had reached the last ditch in his fight for survival. Leaving his little less miserable brothers and sisters, he walked once round me, and then curled himself up between my big feet. When I picked him up and put him inside my coat—it was a bitterly cold morning—he tried to show his gratitude by licking my face, and I tried to show him I was not aware of his appalling stench.

He was rising three months then, and I bought him for fifteen rupees. He is rising thirteen years now, and all the gold in India would not buy him.

When I got him home, and he had made his first acquaintance with a square meal, warm water, and soap, we scrapped his kenneled name of Pincha and rechristened him Robin, in memory of a faithful old collie who had saved my young brother, aged four, and myself, aged six, from the attack of an infuriated she-bear.

Robin responded to regular meals as parched land does to rain, and after he had been with us for a few weeks, acting on the principle that a boy's and a pup's training cannot be started too early, I took him out one morning, intending to get a little away from him and fire a shot or two to get him used to the sound of gunfire.

At the lower end of our estate there are some dense thorn bushes, and while I was skirting round them a peafowl got up, and forgetting all about Robin, who is following at heel, I brought the bird fluttering down. It landed in the thorn bushes and Robin dashed in after it. The bushes were too thick and thorny for me to enter them, so I ran round to the far side where beyond the bushes was open ground, and beyond that again heavy tree and grass jungle which I knew the wounded bird would make for. The open ground was flooded with morning sunlight, and if I had been armed with a movie camera I should have had an opportunity of securing a unique picture. The peafowl, an old hen, with neck feathers stuck out at right angles, and one wing broken, was making for the tree jungle, while Robin, with stern to the ground, was hanging on to her tail and being dragged along. Running forward I very foolishly caught the bird by the neck and lifted it clear of the ground, whereon it promptly lashed out with both legs, and sent Robin heels-over-head. In a second he was up and on his feet again, and when I laid the dead bird down, he danced round it making little dabs alternately at its head and tail. The lesson was over for that morning, and as we returned home it would have been difficult to say which of us was the more proud—Robin, at bringing home his first bird, or I, at having picked a winner out of a filthy basket. The shooting season was now drawing to a close, and for the next few days Robin was not given anything larger than quail, doves, and an occasional partridge to retrieve.

We spent the summer on the hills, and on our annual migration to the foothills in November, at the end of a long fifteen-mile march as we turned a sharp corner, one of a big troop of langurs jumped off the hillside and crossed the road a few inches in front of Robin's nose. Disregarding my whistle, Robin dashed down the khudside, after the langur, which promptly sought safety in a tree. The ground was open with a few trees here and there, and after going steeply down for thirty or forty yards flattened out for a few yards before going sharply down into the valley below. On the right-hand side of this flat ground there were a few bushes with a deep channel scoured out by rain-water running through them. Robin had hardly entered these bushes when he was out again, and with ears laid back and tail tucked in was running for dear life, with an enormous leopard bounding after him and gaining on him at every bound. I was unarmed and all the assistance I could render was to 'Ho' and 'Har' at the full extent of my lungs. The men carrying M.'s dandy joined in lustily, the pandemonium reaching its climax when the hundred or more langurs added their alarm-calls, in varying keys. For twenty-five or thirty yards the desperate and unequal race continued, and just as the leopard was within reach of Robin, it unaccountably swerved and disappeared into the valley, while Robin circled round a shoulder of the hill and rejoined us on the road. Two very useful lessons Robin learned from his hairbreadth escape, which he never in after-life forgot. First, that it was dangerous to chase langurs, and second that the alarm-call of a langur denoted the presence of a leopard. Robin resumed his training where it had been interrupted in spring, but it soon became apparent that his early neglect and starvation had affected his heart, for he fainted now after the least exertion.

There is nothing more disappointing for a gun dog

than to be left at home when his master goes out, and as bird-shooting was now taboo for Robin, I started taking him with me when I went out after big game. He took to this new form of sport as readily as a duck takes to water, and from then on has accompanied me whenever I have been out with a rifle.

The method we employ is to go out early in the morning, pick up the tracks of a leopard or tiger, and follow them. When the pug marks can be seen, I do the tracking, and when the animal we are after takes to the jungle, Robin does the tracking. In this way we have on occasion followed an animal for miles before coming up with it.

When shooting on foot, it is very much easier to kill an animal outright than when shooting down on it from a machan, or from the back of an elephant. For one thing, when wounded animals have to be followed up on foot, chance shots are not indulged in, and for another, the vital parts are more accessible when shooting on the same level as the animal than when shooting down on it.

However, even after exercising the greatest care over the shot, I have sometimes only wounded leopard and tigers, who have rampaged round before being quieted by a second or third shot, and only once during all the years that we have shot together has Robin left me in a tight corner. When he rejoined me after his brief absence that day, we decided that the incident was closed and would never be referred to again, but we are older now and possibly less sensitive, anyway Robin—who has exceeded the canine equivalent of three-score-years-and-ten, and who lies at my feet as I write, on a bed he will never again leave—has with a smile from his wise brown eyes and a

wag of his small stump of a tail given me permission to go
ahead and tell you the story.

We did not see the leopard until it stepped clear of the
thick undergrowth and, coming to a stand, looked back
over its left shoulder.

He was an outsized male with a beautiful dark glossy
coat, the rosettes on his skin standing out like clear-cut
designs on a rich velvet ground. I had an unhurried shot
with an accurate rifle at his right shoulder, at the short
range of fifteen yards. By how little I missed his heart
makes no matter, and while the bullet was kicking up the
dust fifty yards away he was high in the air, and, turning
a somersault, landed in the thick undergrowth he had a
minute before left. For twenty, forty, fifty yards we heard
him crashing through the cover, and then the sound
ceased as abruptly as it had begun. This sudden cessation
of sound could be accounted for in two ways: either the
leopard had collapsed and died in his tracks, or fifty yards
away he had reached open ground.

We had walked far that day; the sun was near setting
and we were still four miles from home. This part of the
jungle was not frequented by man, and there was not one
chance in a million of anyone passing that way by night,
and last, and the best reason of all for leaving the leopard, I was unarmed and could neither be left alone nor
taken along to follow up the wounded animal—so we
turned to the north and made for home. There was no
need for me to mark the spot, for I had walked through
these jungles by day—and often by night—for near on
half a century, and could have found my way blindfolded
to any part of them.

Night had only just given place to day the following

morning when Robin—who had not been with us the previous evening—and I arrived at the spot I had fired from. Very warily Robin, who was leading, examined the ground where the leopard had stood, and then raising his head and snuffing the air he advanced to the edge of the undergrowth, where the leopard in falling had left great splashes of blood. There was no need for me to examine the blood to determine the position of the wound, for at the short range I had fired at I had seen the bullet strike, and the spurt of dust on the far side was proof that the bullet had gone right through the leopard's body.

It might be necessary later on to follow up the blood trail, but just at present a little rest after our four-mile walk in the dark would do no harm, and might on the other hand prove of great value to us. The sun was near rising, and at that early hour of the morning all the jungle folk were on the move, and it would be advisable to hear what they had to say on the subject of the wounded animal before going further.

Under a near-by tree I found a dry spot to which the saturating dew had not penetrated, and with Robin stretched out at my feet had finished my cigarette when a chital hind, and then a second and a third, started calling some sixty yards to our left front. Robin sat up and slowly turning his head looked at me, and on catching my eye, as slowly turned back in the direction of the calling deer. He had traveled far along the road of experience since that day he had first heard the alarm-call of a langur, and he knew now—as did every bird and animal within hearing— that the chital were warning the jungle folk of the presence of a leopard.

From the manner in which the chital were calling it

was evident that the leopard was in full view of them. A little more patience and they would tell us if he was alive. They had been calling for about five minutes when suddenly, and all together, they called once and again, and then settled down to their regular call; the leopard was alive and had moved, and was now quiet again. All that we needed to know was the position of the leopard, and this information we could get by stalking the chital.

Moving down-wind for fifty yards we entered the thick undergrowth, and started to stalk the deer—not a difficult task, for Robin can move through any jungle as silently as a cat, and long practice has taught me where to place my feet. The chital were not visible until we were within a few feet of them. They were standing in the open and looking towards the north in the exact direction, as far as I was able to judge, in which the crashing sound of the evening before had ceased.

Up to this point the chital had been of great help to us; they had told us the leopard was lying out in the open and that it was alive, and they had now given us the direction. It had taken us the best part of an hour to acquire this information, and if the chital now caught sight of us and warned the jungle folk of our presence, they would in one second undo the good they had so far done. I was debating whether it would be better to retrace our steps and work down below the calling deer and try to get a shot from behind them, or move them from our vicinity by giving the call of a leopard, when one of the hinds turned her head and looked straight into my face. Next second, with a cry of 'Ware man,' they dashed away at top speed. I had only about five yards to cover to reach the open ground, but quick as I was the leopard was quicker, and I was only in time to see his hind quarters and tail disappearing behind some bushes. The chital had very effectively spoilt my chance of a shot, and the leopard would now have to be relocated and marked down all over again—this time by Robin.

I stood on the open ground for some minutes, to give the leopard time to settle down and the scent he had left in his passage to blow past us, and then took Robin due west across the track of the wind, which was blowing from the north. We had gone about sixty or seventy yards when Robin, who was leading, stopped and turned to face into the wind. Robin is mute in the jungles, and has a wonderful control over his nerves. There is one nerve, however, running down the back of his hind legs, which he cannot control when he is looking at a leopard, or when the scent of a leopard is warm and strong. This nerve was now twitching, and agitating the long hair on the upper part of his hind legs.

A very violent cyclonic storm had struck this part of the forest the previous summer, uprooting a number of trees; it was towards one of these fallen trees, forty yards from where we were standing, that Robin was now looking. The branches were towards us, and on either side of the trunk there were light bushes and few scattered tufts of short grass.

At any other time Robin and I would have made straight for our quarry; but on this occasion a little extra caution was advisable. Not only were we dealing with an animal who when wounded knows no fear, but in addition we were dealing with a leopard who had had fifteen hours in which to nurse his grievance against man, and who could in consequence be counted on to have all his fighting instincts thoroughly aroused.

When leaving home that morning I had picked up the .275 rifle I had used the previous evening. A good rifle to carry when miles have to be covered, but not the weapon one would select to deal with a wounded leopard; so instead of a direct approach, I picked a line that would take us fifteen yards from, and parallel to, the fallen tree. Step by step, Robin leading, we moved along this line, and had passed the branches and were opposite the trunk when Robin stopped. Taking the direction from him, I presently saw what had attracted his attention—the tip of the leopard's tail slowly raised, and as slowly lowered—the warning a leopard invariably gives before charging. Pivoting to the right on my heels, I had just got the rifle to my shoulder when the leopard burst through the intervening bushes and sprang at us. My bullet, fired more with the object of deflecting him than with any hope of killing or even hitting him, passed under his belly and went through the fleshy part of his left thigh. The crack of the rifle, more than the wound, had the effect of deflecting the leopard sufficiently to make him pass my right shoulder without touching me, and before I could get in another shot, he disappeared into the bushes beyond.

Robin had not moved from my feet, and together we now examined the ground the leopard had passed over. Blood we found in plenty, but whether it had come from the old wounds torn open by the leopard's violent exertions, or from my recent shot it was impossible to say. Anyway it made no difference to Robin, who without a moment's hesitation took up the trail. After going through some very heavy cover we came on knee-high undergrowth, and had proceeded about a couple of hundred yards when I saw the leopard get up in front of us, and before I could get the rifle to bear on him, he disappeared under a lantana bush. This bush with its branches resting on the ground was as big as a cottage tent, and in addition to affording the leopard ideal cover gave him all the advantages for launching his next attack.

Robin and I had come very well out of our morning's adventure and it would have been foolish now, armed as I was, to pursue the leopard further, so without more ado we turned about and made for home.

Next morning we were back on the ground. From a very early hour Robin had been agitating to make a start, and, ignoring all the interesting smells the jungle holds in the morning, would have made me do the four miles at a run had that been possible.

I had armed myself with a 450/400, and was in consequence feeling much happier than I had done the previous day. When we were several hundred yards from the lantana bush, I made Robin slow down and advance cautiously, for it is never safe to assume that a wounded animal will be found where it has been left hours previous as the following regrettable incident shows.

A sportsman of my acquaintance wounded a tiger one afternoon, and followed the blood trail for several miles along a valley. Next morning, accompanied by a number of men, one of whom was carrying his empty rifle and leading the way, he set out intending to take up the tracking where he had left off. His way led over the previous day's blood trail, and while still a mile from the spot where the tiger had been left, the leading man, who incidentally was the local shikari, walked on to the wounded tiger and was killed. The rest of the party escaped, some by climbing trees and others by showing a clean pair of heels.

I had marked the exact position of the lantana bush, and now took Robin along a line that would pass a few yards on the lee side of it. Robin knew all that was worth knowing about this method of locating the position of an animal by cutting across the wind, and we had only gone a short distance, and were still a hundred yards from the bush, when he stopped, turned and faced into the wind, and communicated to me that he could smell the leopard. As on the previous day, he was facing a fallen tree which was lying along the edge of, and parallel to, the thick undergrowth through which we had followed the leopard to the lantana bush after he had charged us. On our side of the tree the ground was open, but on the far side there was a dense growth of waist-high basonta bushes. Having signaled to Robin to carry on along our original line, we went past the lantana bush, in which he showed no interest, to a channel washed out by rain-water. Here, removing my coat, I filled it with as many stones as the stitches would hold, and with this improvised sack slung over my shoulder returned to the open ground near the tree.

Resuming my coat, and holding the rifle ready for instant use, I took up a position fifteen yards from the tree and started throwing the stones, first on to the tree and then into the bushes on the far side of it with the object of making the leopard—assuming he was still alive—charge on to the open ground where I could deal with him. When all my ammunition was exhausted I coughed, clapped my hands, and shouted, and neither during the bombardment nor after it did the leopard move or make any sound to indicate that he was alive.

I should now have been justified in walking straight up to the tree and looking on the far side of it, but remembering an old jungle saying, "It is never safe to assume that a leopard is dead until it has been skinned," I set out to circle round the tree, intending to reduce the size of the circles until I could see right under the branches and along the whole length of the trunk. I made the radius of the first circle about twenty-five yards, and had gone two-thirds of the way round when Robin stopped. As I looked down to see what had attracted his attention, there were a succession of deep-throated, angry grunts, and the leopard made straight for us. All I could see was the undergrowth being violently agitated in a direct line towards us, and I only just had time to swing half right and bring the rifle up, when the head and shoulders of the leopard appeared out of the bushes a few feet away.

The leopard's spring and my shot were simultaneous, and side stepping to the left and leaning back as far as I could I fired the second barrel from my hip into his side as he passed me.

When a wounded animal, be he leopard or tiger, makes a headlong charge and fails to contact he invariably carries on and does not return to the attack until he is again disturbed.

I had side-stepped to the left to avoid crushing Robin, and when I looked down for him now, he was nowhere to be seen. For the first time in all the years we had hunted together we had parted company in a tight corner, and he was now probably trying to find his way home, with very little chance of being able to avoid the many dangers that lay before him in the intervening four miles of jungle. Added to the natural dangers he would have to face in a jungle with which, owing to its remoteness from home, he was not familiar, was the weak condition of his heart.

It was therefore with great misgivings that I turned about to go in search of him, and as I did so, I caught sight of his head projecting from behind a tree trunk at the edge of a small clearing a hundred yards away. When I raised my hand and beckoned, he disappeared into the undergrowth, but a little later, with drooped eyes and drooping ears, he crept silently to my feet. Laying down the rifle I picked him up in my arms and, for the second time in his life, he licked my face—telling me as he did so, with little throaty sounds, how glad he was to find me unhurt, and how terribly ashamed he was of himself for having parted company from me.

Our reactions to the sudden and quite unexpected danger that had confronted us were typical of how a canine and a human being act in an emergency, when the danger that threatens is heard, and not seen. In Robin's case it had impelled him to seek safety in silent and rapid retreat; whereas in my case it had the effect of gluing my feet to the ground and making retreat—rapid or otherwise—impossible.

When I had satisfied Robin that he was not to blame for our temporary separation, and his small body had stopped trembling, I put him down and together we walked up to where the leopard, who had put up such a game fight, and had so nearly won the last round was lying dead.

I have told you the story, and while I have been telling it Robin—the biggest-hearted and most faithful friend man ever had—has gone to the Happy Hunting Grounds, where I know I shall find him waiting for me.

Jim Corbett unwittingly reveals so much about himself in "Robin" that I have left telling you something about him until the end of his story. Corbett was a great big-game hunter, surely one of the greatest who ever lived. Far more than that, he was a great man, a man humbled by the nobility of the common people of India, around whom he chose to live. Conversely, no one commanded more respect from the native people than Corbett. Together, and over the years, they journeyed over a long, often dangerous, road. For tens upon tens of thousands of poor village people, Corbett was their greatest hero and their protector. For them he staked his own life, repeatedly, hunting and killing man-eating tigers and leopards that had taken countless lives. The enormous danger to himself was of little consequence to Corbett, who alone was able to end the terror imposed upon entire regions by marauding maneaters and he saw this as his unquestioned duty. His own words—the last in his most famous autobiography, Man-Eaters of Kumaon, *published in 1946—say it best: "There have been occasions when life has hung by a thread and others when a light purse and disease resulting from exposure and strain have made the going difficult, but for all these occasions I am amply rewarded if my hunting has resulted in saving one human life."*

Born in 1875 in Naini Tal, Corbett was the twelfth of seventeen natural and adopted children of British parents. To say his was a large family is an understatement, and the fact that is was a happy and wholesome one is exceptional. Corbett lived all his life with one of his sisters, Maggie. Neither ever married, in part due to the fact that they had chosen to care for their mother until her death, which happened long after Corbett and Maggie were past marrying age. However, Corbett's discreet, long-time affair with a married woman was the better part of the reason why he remained a life-long bachelor. He was a successful businessman and landowner who worked for government and the railroad for many years. At the end of his life, he was universally considered one of the greatest conservationists of his day. Corbett National Park, the largest conservation area in India, was dedicated in his honor.

Corbett's books have remained extremely popular since they were first published in England, and afterwards were reprinted by a number of publishing houses. In his small book, Treetops, Corbett describes guiding a young, newly-married woman and her husband on a photographic expedition deep into the jungle. They stayed overnight at Treetops, a large tree house built high up and away from danger. Corbett, then in his seventies, slept on the floor at the top of the ladder, in the event a wild animal presented danger. In the morning, a motor escort came for the couple. They were met with sad news that the young woman's beloved father had died during that night at Treetops. Corbett later wrote, "For the first time in the history of the world a young girl climbed into a tree one day a Princess, and after having what she described as her most thrilling experience she climbed down from the tree the next day a Queen—God Bless her." The woman Corbett spoke of was Queen Elizabeth of England.

And yet I believe Corbett would allow that of all the remarkable times in his life, the one he would hold closest to his heart was that period he spent with a small spaniel he called Robin, his most devoted and beloved friend.

Your Boy and His Dog

By Robert Benchley

From *Chips Off the Old Benchley* By Robert Benchley.
Copyright 1932 by Liberty Magazine.
By permission of Harper & Brothers.

"The ideal age for a boy to own a dog is between forty-five and fifty," explains Robert Benchley in "Your Boy and His Dog," and it's classic Benchley that he then suggests a course of training that's more likely to result in the dog training the boy.

Benchley was a regular of the Algonquin Round Table, along with Groucho and Harpo Marx, Will Rogers, and notable others who entertained America in print and on stage during the "Roaring Twenties." They lunched at the Algonquin Hotel in Manhattan's theater district and fed one another witty gossip. "Did you hear Dorothy's latest?" someone would snigger about writer Dorothy Parker, the infamous female member of the Round Table. "A real estate agent was showing her an apartment for rent and she protested, 'Oh, dear, that's much too big. All I need is room enough to lay a hat and a few friends.' "

Benchley never wanted to be, but was "America's greatest humorist of the century." Of his singular style he shrugged, "I don't know enough words to have a style. I know, at the most, fifteen adjectives."

"Everybody wanted to be his close friend, and to be with him all the time," Frank Sullivan wrote, "and he, kindly and gregarious man that he was, would have liked to oblige. But there simply was not enough Benchley to go around." So personable a man was Benchley that he even endeared himself to his bank, even when his account was mired in red. He'd endorse his checks, "Dear Banker's Trust, I love you. Bob," and "Having a wonderful time, wish you were here."

Benchley wrote for Life *and* Vanity Fair *and shared an office with Mrs. Parker, who was described by Alexander Woollcott as "a blend of Little Nell and Lady Macbeth." Parker and Benchley's cable address was "Park-bench," the sign on their office door: Utica Drop Forge & Tool Company,*

Robert Benchley, President. Dorothy Parker, President. Their office was so small that Benchley remarked, "If it were any smaller, it would have constituted adultery." Restless when no one came to see them, Mrs. Parker changed the sign to Men.

Life and yes, even dogs, overwhelmed Benchley, as you'll find out in "Your Boy and His Dog."

People are constantly asking me: "What kind of dog shall I give my boy?" or sometimes: "What kind of boy shall I give my dog?" And although we are always somewhat surprised to get a query like this, ours really being the Jam and Fern Question Box, we usually give the same answer to both forms of inquiry: "Are you quite sure that you want to do either?" This confuses them, and we are able to snatch a few more minutes for our regular work.

But the question of Boy and Dog is one which will not be downed. There is no doubt that every healthy, normal boy (if there is such a thing in these days of Child Study) should own a dog at some time in his life, preferably between the ages of forty-five and fifty. Give a dog to a boy who is much younger and his parents will find them-selves obliged to pack up and go to the Sailors' Snug Harbor to live until the dog runs away—which he will do as soon as the first pretty face comes along.

But a dog teaches a boy fidelity, perseverance, and to turn around three times before lying down—very impor-tant traits in times like these. In fact, just as soon as a dog comes along who, in addition to these qualities, also knows when to buy and sell stocks, he can be moved right up to the boy's bedroom and the boy can sleep in the dog house. In buying a dog for a very small child, attention must be paid to one or two essential points. In the first place, the dog must be one which will come apart easily or of such a breed that the sizing will get pasty and all gummed up when wet. Dachshunds are ideal dogs for small children, as they are already stretched and pulled to such a length that the child cannot do much harm one way or the other. The dachshund being so long also makes it difficult for a very small child to go through with the favorite juvenile maneuver of lifting the dog's hind legs up in the air and wheeling it along like a barrow, cooing, "Diddyap!" Any small child trying to lift a dachshund's hind legs up very high is going to find itself flat on its back.

For the very small child who likes to pick animals up around the middle and carry them over to the fireplace, mastiffs, St. Bernards, or Russian wolfhounds are not indicated—that is, not if the child is of any value at all. It is not that the larger dogs resent being carried around the middle and dropped in the fireplace (in fact, the smaller the dog, the more touchy it is in matters of dignity, as is so often the case with people and nations); but, even though a mastiff does everything that it can to help the child in carrying it by the diaphragm, there are matters of gravity to be reckoned with which make it impossible to carry the thing through without something being broken. If a dog could be trained to wrestle and throw the child immediately, a great deal of time could be saved.

But, as we have suggested, the ideal age for a boy to own a dog is between forty-five and fifty. By this time the boy ought to have attained his full growth and, provided he is ever going to, ought to know more or less what he wants to make of himself in life. At this age the dog will be more of a companion than a chattel, and, if necessary, can be counted upon to carry the boy by the middle and drop him into bed in case sleep overcomes him at a dinner or camp meeting or anything. It can also be counted upon to tell him he has made a fool of himself and embarrassed all his friends. A wife could do no more.

The training of the dog is something which should be left to the boy, as this teaches him responsibility and accustoms him to the use of authority, probably the only time he will ever have a chance to use it. If, for example, the dog insists on following the boy when he is leaving the house, even after repeated commands to "Go on back home!" the boy must decide on one of two courses. He must either take the dog back to the house and lock it in the cellar, or, as an alternate course, he can give up the idea of going out himself and stay with the dog. The latter is the better way, especially if the dog is in good voice and given to screaming the house down.

There has always been considerable difference of opinion as to whether a dog really thinks. I, personally, have no doubt that distinct mental processes do go on inside the dog's brain, although many times these processes are hardly worthy of the name. I have known dogs, especially puppies, who were almost as stupid as humans in their mental reactions.

The only reason that puppies do not get into more trouble than they do (if there *is* any more trouble than that which puppies get into) is that they are so small. A child, for instance, should not expect to be able to fall as heavily, eat as heartily of shoe leather, or throw up as casually as a puppy does, for there is more bulk to a child and the results of these practices will be more serious in exact proportion to the size and capacity. Whereas, for example, a puppy might be able to eat only the toe of a slipper, a child might well succeed in eating the whole shoe—which, considering the nails and everything, would not be wise.

One of the reasons why dogs are given credit for serious thinking is the formation of their eyebrows. A dog lying in front of a fire and looking up at his master may appear pathetic, disapproving, sage, or amused, according to the angle at which its eyebrows are set by nature.

It is quite possible, and even probable, that nothing at all is going on behind the eyebrows. In fact, one dog who had a great reputation for sagacity once told me in confidence that most of the time when he was supposed to be regarding a human with an age-old philosophical rumination he was really asleep behind his shaggy overhanging brows. "You could have knocked me over with a feather," he said, "when I found out that people were talking about my wisdom and suggesting running me for President."

This, of course, offers a possibility for the future of the child itself. As soon as the boy makes up his mind just what type of man he wants to be, he could buy some crepe hair and a bottle of spirit gum and make himself a pair of eyebrows to suit the role: converging toward the nose if he wants to be a judge or savant; pointing upward from the edge of the eyes if he wants to be a worried-looking man, like a broker; elevated to his forehead if he plans on simulating surprise as a personal characteristic; and in red patches if he intends being a stage Irishman.

In this way he may be able to get away with a great deal, as his pal the dog does.

At any rate, the important thing is to get a dog for the boy and see what each can teach the other. The way things are going now with our Younger Generation, the chances are that before long the dog will be smoking, drinking gin, and wearing a soft hat pulled over one eye.

Being A Public Character

By Don Marquis

From *Revolt of the Oyster.*
Copyright 1922 by Doubleday & Co.

"What a deeply humorous man Don is, and far closer to Mark Twain than anybody I know or am ever likely to know," columnist Franklin P. Anderson wrote. But Marquis would lament, "It would be one on me if I should be remembered longest for creating a cockroach character." This cockroach hammered out prose on a typewriter by striking a key at a time with his head. His name was Archy. Archy's muse was an alley cat named Mehitabel. There was a human appeal about this unlikely pair. And thus, "Archy & Mehitabel," one of the most popular columns of its day, took its rightful place in the annals of 19th century literary humor:

> *expression is the need of my soul*
> *i was once a vers libre bard*
> *but i died and my soul went into the body of*
> *a cockroach*
> *it has given me a new outlook upon life*
> *i see things from the under side now*
> *thank you for the apple peelings in your*
> *wastebasket*

Famous writers during the Depression were lured by big bucks to Hollywood, where they'd create screenplays for a staggering $2,000 a week. Marquis was one. This letter, to Corey Ford, provides exquisite insight into the man and his times:

Dear Mr. Ford:

Sometimes a word will lift gobs of gloom from a struggling spirit. At the present moment I worship you.

Have thrown away in despair three stories in the last month. It began to seem to me that there must have been some mistake—and that after all, I couldn't write a humorous spiel. There had been, somehow, a series of damned accidents; I had been kidding myself; but now I was about to be found-out.

Then I happened to pick up Vanity Fair *for April and your discussion of comedy... "Don Marquis, of course..." you say, has humour.*

That "of course" has saved my life (whatever that is worth). If you had just said I had humour, it would not have been half the uplift—but the "of course" did the trick... I began at once to recapture the sense of myself as a hell of a fellow; it had all oozed away, that sense. It was like—of course, there is the Washington Monument... of course, there's the Atlantic Ocean—of course, there's the Atlantic Ocean—of course, there's the circulation of the blood—you know what I mean; I felt established, by the casual, confident, quality of that "of course." I quit crying in my beer for the first time in weeks, and said: "Good? Of course I'm good. Here's a bird with some sense; he knows it, you're goddamn right I'm good!"

This is a hell of a place out here. It is a country that has never been thought in, and you feel it. It is everywhere commonplace; and nowhere real. It has got me not only licked, but almost annihilated. Quite seriously, your casual and assured "of course" came fluttering like a golden butterfly down the dank alley of my mind. It doesn't seem, to you, so much that I should make a fuss about it, I know, and yet if you're pleased and helped at one of those really critical times that all writers experience, why not say so, even volubly?

Do you know this country? I was never here before November. It is a terrible place. Entirely physical. Full of strange liars. Crowded and empty. Full of banal sunshine and without warmth. It thinks physical fact is an idea in itself, but for all that it is queerly lacking in vigor, even physical vigor. Full of cults that will never have any fruition in actuality. There is a thinness about it that oppresses like the smothering thickness of a nightmare; oppresses the breathing, or starves it. I do not think the women have any milk in their teats.

But I suppose it is more myself than the country; I've been ill.

Yours sincerely,
Don Marquis
Hollywood, California
April 23, 1936

Marquis never let his illness, or the burden of his utterly tragic life, adversely affect his writing. "Being a Public Character," is from a dog's point of view, just as the Archy and Mehitabel columns are about life from a cockroach's. Maybe it was easier for him to deal with life that way. He surely made it a lot easier for us to understand.

Ever since I bit a circus lion, believing him to be another dog, only larger, I've been what Doc Watson calls a Public Character in our town.

Freckles, my boy, was a kind of Public Character, too. All the other boys and dogs in town sort of looked up to him and thought how lucky he was to belong to a dog like me. And he deserved all the glory he got out of it. For if I do say it myself, there's not a dog in town got a better boy than my boy Freckles. I'll back him against any dog's boy anywhere near his size for fighting, swimming, climbing, foot-racing or throwing stones farthest or straightest. Or I'll back him against any stray boy, either.

Well, some dogs may be born Public Characters and like it. And some may be brought up to like it. But with me, becoming a Public Character happened all in a flash, and it was sort of hard for me to get used to it. One day I was just a private sort of dog. And the next day I had bit that lion and fame came so sudden I scarcely knew how to act.

Even Heinie Hassenyager, the butcher, got stuck on me after I got to be a Public Character. Heinie would come two blocks up Main Street with lumps of Hamburg steak, which is some kind one has already chewed for you, and give them to me. Steak, mind you, not old gristly scraps. And before I became a Public Character Heinie even begrudged me the bones I would drag out of the box under his counter when he wasn't looking.

My daily hope was that I could live up to it all. I had always tried, before I happened to bite that lion, to be a friendly kind of dog towards boys and humans and dogs, all three. I'd always been expected to do a certain amount of tail-wagging and be friendly. But as soon as I got to be a Public Character, I saw right away that I wasn't expected to be *too* friendly any more.

So when Heinie would bring me the ready-chewed steak I'd growl at him a little bit. And then I'd bolt and gobble the steak like I didn't think so darned much of it and was doing Heinie a big favor to eat it. That way of acting made a big hit with Heinie, too. I could see that he was honored and flattered because I didn't go any further than just a growl. And the more I growled, the more steak he brought. Everybody in town fed me. I pretty near ate myself to death for awhile, besides all the meat I buried back of Doc Watson's store to dig up later.

The worst of it was that people, after a week or so, began to expect me to pull something else remarkable. Freckles, he got up a circus, and charged pins and marbles, and cents, when he found anyone that had any, to get into it, and I was the principal part of that circus. I was in a cage. I didn't care for being caged and circused that way myself. And it was right at that circus that considerable trouble started.

Seeing me in a cage like that, all famoused-up, with more meat poked through the slats than two dogs could eat, made Mutt Mulligan and some of my old friends jealous. Mutt, he nosed by the cage and sniffed. I nosed a piece of meat out of the cage to him. Mutt grabbed it and gobbled it down, but he didn't thank me any. Mutt, he says:

"There's a new dog downtown that says he blew in from Chicago. He says he used to be a Blind Man's Dog on a street corner there. He's a pretty wise dog, and he's a right ornery-looking dog, too. He's peeled considerably where he has been bit in fights.

"You got such a swell head on you the last week or so that you gotta be licked. You can fool boys and humans all you want to about that accidental old lion, but us dogs got your number all right. What that Blind Man's Dog from Chicago would do to you would be a plenty!"

"Well then," I says, "I'll be out of this cage about supper time. Suppose you bring that Blind Man's Dog around here. And if he ain't got a spiked collar on him, I'll fight him. I won't fight a spiked-collared dog to please anybody."

And I wouldn't neither, without I had one on myself.

If you can't get a dog by the throat or the back of his neck, what's the use of fighting him? You might just as well try to eat a blacksmith shop as fight one of those spike-collared dogs.

Well, that night after supper, along comes the Blind Man's Dog. Never did I see a Blind Man's Dog that was as tight-skinned. I had been used to fighting loose-skinned dogs that you can get some sort of a reasonable hold on while you are working around for position. And running into a tight-skinned dog that way, all of a sudden and all unprepared for it, would make anybody nervous.

Lots of dogs wouldn't have fought him at all when they realized how they had been fooled about him, and how tight-skinned he was. But I was a Public Character now, and I had to fight him. More than that, I ain't ready to say yet that that dog actually licked me. Freckles he hit him with a lump of soft coal, and he got all off me and run away before I could get my second wind. There's no telling what I would have done to that Blind Man's Dog, tight-skinned as he was, if he hadn't run away before I got my second wind.

Well, there's some mighty peculiar dogs in this world, let alone boys and humans. The word got around town, in spite of his running away before I got my second wind, that the Blind Man's Dog had actually licked me! Every time Freckles and me went down the street some one would say:

"Well, the dog that licked the lion got licked himself, did he?"

And if it was a lady said it, Freckles would spit on the sidewalk through the place where his front teeth are out and pass on politely as if he hadn't heard and say nothing. And if it was a man that said it Freckles would thumb his nose at him. And if it was a girl, he would rub a handful of sand into her hair. And if it was a boy anywhere his size, there would be a fight. If it was too big a boy, Freckles would sling railroad iron at him.

I didn't care so awful much for myself, but I hated it for Freckles. For one Saturday afternoon when there wasn't any school, instead of going swimming with the other kids or playing baseball, or anything, he went and played with girls. He must have been pretty well down-hearted and felt himself pretty much of an outcast, or he wouldn't have done that. I am an honest dog, and the truth must be told, the disgrace along with everything else, and the truth is that he played with girls of his own accord that day. Any boy will play with girls when all the boys and girls are playing together; but no boy is going to go off alone and look up a bunch of girls and play with them unless he has had considerable of a downfall.

Right next to our side of the yard was the Wilkinses. Freckles was sitting on the top of their fence when the three Wilkins girls came out to play. There was only two boys in the Wilkins family, and they were twins; but they were only year-old babies and didn't amount to anything. The two oldest Wilkins girls each had one of the twins taking care of it. And the other Wilkins girl had one of those big dolls made as big as a baby. They were rolling those babies and the doll around the grass in a wheelbarrow, and the wheel came off, and that's how Freckles happened to go over.

"Up in the attic" says one, when he had fixed up the wheelbarrow, "there's a little old express wagon with one wheel off that would be better'n this wheelbarrow. Maybe you could fix that wheel on, too."

Freckles, he fell for it. After he got the wagon fixed, they got to playing charades and fool girl games like that. The hired girl was off for the afternoon, and pretty soon Mrs. Wilkins hollered up the stairs that she was going to be gone for an hour, and to take good care of the twins, and then we were alone in the place.

Well, it wasn't much fun for me. They played and they played and I stuck to Freckles. I stuck to him because a dog should stick to his boy, and a boy should stick to his dog, no matter what the disgrace. But after a while I got pretty tired and lay down on a rug, and a new kind of flea struck me. After I had chased him down and cracked him with my teeth I went to sleep.

I must have slept pretty sound and pretty long. All of a sudden I waked up with a start and almost choking, for the place was smoky. I barked and no one answered.

The house was on fire, and it looked like I was alone in it. I went down the back stairway but the door that led out on the first floor landing was locked and I had to go up again. By the time I got back up, the front stairway was a great deal fuller of smoke, and I could see glints of flame through it way down below. But it was the only way out of the place.

On the top step I stumbled over a gray wool bunch of something or other, and I picked it up in my mouth. Think I, "That's Freckle's gray sweater that he is so stuck on. I might as well take it down to him."

I got kind of confused and excited. And it struck me all of a sudden, by the time I was down to the second floor, that the sweater weighed an awful lot. I dropped it on the second floor, and ran into one of the front bedrooms and looked out.

The whole town was in the front yard and in the street. And in the midst of the crowd was Mrs. Wilkins, carrying on like mad. "My baby!" she yelled. "Save my baby. Let me loose! I'm going after my baby!"

I stood up on my hind legs, with my head just out of that bedroom window, and the flame and smoke licking up all around me, and barked. "My doggie! My doggie!" yells Freckles who was in the crowd. And he made a run for the house, but someone grabbed him and slung him back.

And Mrs. Wilkins made a run, but they held her, too. Old Pop Wilkins, Mrs. Wilkins's husband, was jumping up and down in from of Mrs. Wilkins yelling, here was her baby. He had a real baby on one arm and that big doll in the other, and was so excited he thought he had both babies. Later I heard what happened. The kids had thought that they were getting out with both twins but one of them had saved the doll and left a twin behind.

Well, I thinks that the baby will likely turn up in the crowd, and I'd better get out of here myself while the getting was good. I ran out of the bedroom, and run into that hunched-up gray bundle again.

I ain't saying I knew it was the missing twin in a gray shawl when I picked it up a second time. And I ain't saying I didn't know it. The fact is I did pick it up. It may be that I was so rattled I just picked it up because I had had it in my mouth before and didn't quite know what I was doing. But the record is something you can't go behind, and the record is that I got out the back way and into the backyard with that bundle swinging from my mouth, and walked around into the front yard and laid that bundle down—*and it was the twin!*

I don't make any claim that I *knew* it was the twin till

I got into the front yard. But you can't provide I *didn't* know it was. And nobody tried to prove it. The gray bundle let out a squall.

"My baby!" yells Mrs. Wilkins. And she kissed me.

"Three cheers for Spot!" yelled the whole town. And they give them.

And then I saw what the lay of the land was, so I wagged my tail and barked. It called for hero stuff, and I threw my head up and looked noble—and pulled it.

An hour before Freckles and me had been outcasts. And now we was Public Characters again. We walked down Main Street and we owned it. And we hadn't any more got to Doc Watson's drug store than in rushed Heinie Hassenyager with a Hamburg steak, and with tears in his eyes.

"It's got chicken livers mixed in it, too!" says Heinie.

I ate it. But while I ate it, I growled at him.

A Very Shy Gentleman

By P. G. Wodehouse

Copyright 1917, 1945 by P. G. Wodehouse.
Reprinted by the author's agents,
Scott Meredith Literary Agency.

English-born Pelham Grenville Wodehouse, by the end of his life, had written one hundred books about silly aristocratic young Englishmen, empty-headed young ladies, domineering dowagers, pompous peers of the realm, and arrogant men of business. Bertie Wooster, fictitious standard-bearer of the "smart set" of young Edwardian gentlemen-of-means, and Jeeves, his loyal valet and the epitome of a gentleman of the servant class, were Wodehouse's most famous characters. Their riotous misadventures reached their peak during World War II, when the odd twosome's jolly escapades lifted the spirits of a war-torn England. Of steadfast Jeeves, Wodehouse wrote:

"I find it curious to recall how softly and undramatically Jeeves first entered my little world. Characteristically, he did not thrust himself forward. On that occasion, he spoke just two lines.
"The first was:
" 'Mrs. Gregson to see you, sir.'
"The second:
" 'Very good, sir, which suit will you wear?' "

This tone of genteel understatement made Wodehouse's books so appealing, yet during the war his celebrity was seriously tarnished by controversial radio broadcasts he made while being held captive in Berlin in 1941. Pained by accusations, he never returned to England, immigrating to the United States instead, where he died in 1975 at the age of 94. In an almost-too-late, reconciliatory honor for a lifetime of literary achievement, Wodehouse was knighted, shortly before his death, by Queen Elizabeth.

"A Very Shy Gentleman" is narrated by a dog—and it's pure, delicious Wodehouse.

Looking back, I always consider that my career as a dog proper really started when I was bought for the sum of one dollar by the Shy Man. That event marked the end of my puppyhood. The knowledge that I was worth actual cash to somebody filled me with a sense of new responsibilities. It sobered me. Besides, it was only after that dollar changed hands that I went out into the great world; and, however interesting life may be in an Eighth Avenue saloon, it is only when you go out into the world that you really broaden your mind and begin to see things.

Within its limitations, my life had been singularly full and vivid. I was born, as I say, in a saloon on Eighth Avenue, and, however lacking a saloon may be in refinement and the true culture, it certainly provides plenty of excitement. Before I was six weeks old, I had upset three policemen by getting between their legs when they came round to the side door, thinking they had heard suspicious noises; and I can still recall the interesting sensation of being chased seventeen times round the yard with a broom handle after a well-planned and completely successful raid on the free-lunch counter.

These and other happenings of a like nature soothed for the moment, but could not cure the restlessness which has always been so marked a trait in my character. I have always been restless, unable to settle down in one place and anxious to get on to the next thing. This may be due to a gypsy strain in my ancestry—one of my uncles having traveled with a circus—or it may be the artistic temperament, acquired from a grandfather who, before dying of a surfeit of paste in the property-room of the Brunswick (Pa.) Coliseum, which he was visiting in the course of a professional tour, had an established reputation in vaudeville as one of Professor Pond's Performing Poodles.

I owe the fullness and variety of my life to this restlessness of mine, for I have repeatedly left comfortable homes in order to follow some perfect stranger who looked as if he were on his way to somewhere interesting. Sometimes I think I must have cat blood in me.

The Shy Man came into our yard one afternoon in April, while I was sleeping with Mother in the sun on an old sweater which we had borrowed from Fred, one of the bartenders. I heard Mother growl, but I didn't take any notice. Mother is what they call a good watchdog, and she growls at everybody except Master. At first, when she used to do it, I would get up and bark my head off, but not now. Life's too short to bark at everybody who comes into our yard. It is behind the saloon and they keep empty bottles and things there, so people are always coming and going.

Besides, I was tired. I had had a very busy morning, helping the men bring in a lot of cases of beer and running into the saloon to talk to Fred and generally look after things. So I was just dozing off again, when I heard a voice say, "Well, he's ugly enough!" Then I knew that they were talking about me.

I have never disguised it from myself, and nobody has ever disguised it from me, that I am not a handsome dog. Even Mother never thought me beautiful. She was no prize-winning beauty herself, but she never hesitated to criticize my appearance. In fact, I have yet to meet any one who did. The first thing strangers say about me is, "What an ugly dog!"

I don't know what I am. The most of me is terrier. I have a long tail which sticks straight up in the air. My hair is wiry. My eyes are brown. I am jet-black, with a white chest. I once overheard Fred say that was a Swiss-cheese-hound, and I have generally found Fred reliable in his statements.

When I found that I was under discussion, I opened my eyes. Master was standing there, looking down at me, and by his side the man who had just said I was ugly enough. The Man was a thin man, about the age of a bartender and smaller than a policeman. He had patched brown shoes and black trousers.

"But he's got a lovely disposition," said Master.

This was true, luckily for me. Mother always said: "A dog without influence or private means, if he is to make his way in the world, must have either good looks or amiability." But, according to her, I overdid it. "A dog," she used to say, "can have a good heart without chumming with every Tom, Dick and Harry he meets. Your behavior is sometimes quite undog-like." Mother prided herself on being a one-man dog. She kept herself to herself, and wouldn't kiss anybody except Master—not even Fred.

Now, I am a mixer. I can't help it. It's my nature. I like men. I like the taste of their shoes, the smell of their legs, and the sound of their voices. It may be weak of me, but a man has only to speak to me, and a sort of thrill goes right down my spine and sets my tail wagging.

I wagged it now. The Man looked at me rather distantly. He didn't pat me. I suspected—what I afterwards found to be the case—that he was shy; so I jumped up at him, to put him at his ease. Mother growled again. I felt that she did not approve.

"Why, he's took quite a fancy to you already," said Master.

The Man didn't say a word. He was chewing gum, and seemed to be brooding on something. He was one of those silent men. He reminded me of Joe, the old dog down the street at the delicatessen store, who lies at the door all day, blinking and not speaking to anybody.

Master began to talk about me. It surprised me, the way he boosted me. I hadn't a suspicion he admired me so much. From what he said, you would have thought I had won prizes and ribbons down among the swells at the Garden. But the Man didn't seem to be impressed. He kept on chewing gum and saying nothing.

When Master had finished telling him what a wonderful dog I was till I blushed, the Man shifted the gum to one side and spoke.

"Nix on the hot air," he said. "One plunk is my bid, and if he was an angel from on high you couldn't work me for a cent more. What about it?"

A thrill went down my spine and out at my tail, for of course I saw now what was happening. The Man wanted to buy me and take me away. I looked at Master hopefully.

"He's more like a son to me than a dog," said Master, sort of wistful.

"It's his face that makes you feel that way," said the Man, unsympathetically. "If you had a son, that's just how he would look. One plunk is my offer, and I'm in a hurry. What's the answer?"

"You're on," said Master, with a sigh, "though it's giving him away, a valuable dog like that. Where's your dollar?"

The Man got a bit of rope, and tied it round my neck.

I could hear Mother barking advice, and telling me to be a credit to the family, but I was too excited to listen.

"Good-by, Mother," I said. "Good-by, Master. Good-by, Fred. Good-by everybody. I'm off to see life. The Shy Man has bought me for a dollar. Wow!"

I kept running round in circles and shouting, till the Man gave me a kick and told me to quit.

"Cut it out!" he said.

So I did.

I don't know where we went, but it was a mighty long way. I had never been out of our ward before in my life, and I didn't know the whole world was half as big as that. We walked on and on, the Man jerking at my rope whenever I wanted to stop and look at anything. He wouldn't even let me pass the time of day with the dogs we met.

When we had gone about a hundred miles, and were just going to turn in at a dark doorway, a policeman suddenly stopped the Man. I could feel by the way the Man pulled at my rope and tried to hurry on that he didn't want to speak to the policeman. The more I saw of the Man, the more I saw how shy he was.

"Hey!" said the policeman, and we had to stop.

"Say, I got a message for you, Cully," said the policeman.

"It's from the Health Commissioner. He told me to tell you you needed a change of air. See?"

"I get you," said the Man.

"And take it as soon as you like. Else you'll find you'll get it given to you. See?"

I looked at the Man with a good deal of respect. He was evidently some one very important, if they worried so about his health.

"I'm going down to the country tonight," said the Man.

The policeman seemed pleased.

"That's a bit of luck for the country," he said. "Don't go changing your mind."

And he walked on, and we went in at the dark doorway, and climbed about a million stairs and went into a room that smelled of rats. The Man sat down, and swore a little, and chewed his gum, and I sat and looked at him.

Presently I couldn't keep it in any longer.

"Do we live here? Is it true we're going to the country? Wasn't that policeman a good sort? Don't you like policemen? I knew lots of policemen at the saloon. Are there any other dogs here? What is there for dinner? What's in that closet? When are you going to take me out for another run? May I go on the fire escape and see if I can find a cat?"

"Quit that yelping," he said.

"When we go to the country, where shall we live? Are you going to be a caretaker at a house? Fred's father is a caretaker at a big house on Long Island. I've heard Fred talk about it. You didn't meet Fred when you came to the saloon, did you? You would like Fred. Mother likes Fred. We all like Fred."

I was going on to tell him a lot more about Fred, who had always been one of my warmest friends, when he suddenly got hold of a stick and walloped me with it.

"You keep quiet when you're told," he said.

He really was the shyest man I had ever met. It seemed to hurt him to be spoken to. However, he was the boss, and I had to humor him, so I didn't say any more.

We went down to the country that night, just as the Man had told the policeman we would. I was all worked up, for I had heard so much about the country from Fred that I had always wanted to go there. Fred used to go off on a motorcycle sometimes to spend the night with father on Long Island, and once he brought back a squirrel with him, which I thought was for me to eat, but Mother said no. "The first thing a dog has to learn," Mother used often to say, "is that the whole darned world wasn't created for him to eat."

It was quite dark when we got to the country, but the Man seemed to know where to go. He pulled at my rope, and we began to walk along a road with no people in it at all. We walked on and on, but it was all so new to me that I forgot how tired I was. I could feel my mind broadening with every step.

Every now and then we would pass a very big house, which looked as if it was empty, but I knew there was a caretaker inside, because of Fred's father. These big houses belong to very rich people, but they don't live in them till summer, so they put in caretakers, and the caretakers have a dog to keep off burglars. I wondered if that was what I had been brought here for.

"Are you going to be a caretaker?" I asked the Man. "Where are we going? When do we eat?"

"Shut up," he said.

So, I shut up.

After we had been walking a long time, we came to a cottage. A man came out. My Man seemed to know him, for he called him Bill. I was quite surprised to see that the Man was not at all shy with Bill. They seemed to be very friendly.

"Is that him?" said Bill, looking at me.

"Bought him this morning," said the man.

"He's ugly enough," said Bill. "He looks fierce. I guess,

if you want a dog, he's the sort of dog you want. But what do you want one for? It seems to me it's a lot of trouble to take, when there's no need of any trouble at all. What's your kick against doing what I've always wanted to do? What's wrong with just fixing the dog, same as it's always done, and walking in and helping yourself?"

"I'll tell you what's wrong," said the Man. "To start with, you can't get at the dog to fix him except by day, when they let him out. At night he's shut up inside the house. And suppose you fix him during the day, what happens then? Either the guy gets another before night, or else he sits up all night with a gun. It isn't like as if these guys were ordinary ginks. They're down here to look after the house. That's their job, and they aren't taking any chances."

It was the longest speech I had ever hear the Man make, and it seemed to impress Bill. He was quite humble.

"I didn't think of that," he said. "We'd best start in to train this mutt right away."

Mother often used to say, when I went on about wanting to go out into the world and see life, "You'll be sorry when you do. The world isn't all bones and liver." And I hadn't been living with the Man and Bill in their cottage long before I found how right she was.

It was the Man's shyness that made all the trouble. It seemed as if he hated to be taken notice of.

It started on my very first night at the cottage. I had fallen asleep in the kitchen, tired out after all the excitement of the day and the long walks I had had, when something woke me with a start. It was somebody scratching at the window, trying to get in.

Well, I ask you, I ask any dog, what would you have done in my place? Ever since I was old enough to listen, Mother had told me over and over again what I must do in a case like this. It is the A.B.C. of a dog's education. "If you are in a room, and you hear anything trying to get in," Mother used to say, "bark. It may be some one who has business there, or it may not. Bark first, and inquire afterward. Dogs were made to be heard not seen."

I lifted my head and yelled. I have a good, deep voice, due to a hound strain in my pedigree, and, back on Eighth Avenue when there was a full moon, I have often had people leaning out of the windows and saying things for a dozen blocks and more. I took a deep breath and let it go.

"Man!" I shouted. "Bill! Man! Come quick! Here's a burglar getting in!"

Then somebody struck a light, and it was the Man himself. He had come in through the window.

He picked up a stick, and he walloped me. I couldn't understand it. I couldn't see where I had done the wrong thing. But he was the boss, so there was nothing to be said.

If you'll believe me, that same thing happened every night. Every single night! And sometimes twice or three times before morning. And every time I would bark my loudest, and the Man would strike a light and wallop me. The thing was baffling.

I thought it out till my head ached, and finally I got it right. I began to see that Mother's outlook was narrow. No doubt, living with a man like Master at the saloon, a man without a trace of shyness in his composition, barking was all right. But Eighth Avenue is not the world. Circumstances alter cases. I belonged to a man who was a mass of nerves, who went up in the air if you spoke to him. It was up to me to forget the training I had had from Mother, sound as it no doubt was as a general thing, and to adapt myself to the needs of the particular man who had happened to buy me.

So next night, when I heard the window go, I lay there without a word, though it went against all my better feelings. I didn't even growl. Someone came in and moved about in the dark with a lantern, but, though I smelled that it was the Man, I didn't ask him a single question. And presently the Man lit the gas, and came over to me and gave me a pat, which was a thing he had never done before.

"Getting wise, are you?" he said. "Just for that you can have this."

And he let me lick out the saucepan in which the dinner had been cooked.

After that, we got on well. Whenever I heard anyone at the window I just kept curled up and took no notice, and every time I got a bone or something good. It was soft, once you had got the hang of things.

It was about a week after that that the Man took me out one morning, and we walked a long way till we turned in at some big gates, and went along a very smooth road till we came to a great house, standing all by itself in the middle of a whole lot of country.

The Man rang a bell, and the door opened, and an old man came out.

"Well?" he said, not very cordially.

"I thought you might want to buy a good watchdog," said the Man.

"Well, that's darned queer, your saying that," said the caretaker. "It's a coincidence. That's exactly what I do want to buy. I was just thinking of going along and trying to get one. My old dog picked up something this morning that he oughtn't to have, and he's dead, poor feller."

"Poor feller," said the Man. "Found an old bone with phosphorous on it, I guess."

"Maybe. What do you want for this one?"

"Two dollars."

"Is he a good watchdog?"

"Sure he's a good watchdog."

"He looks fierce enough."

"Bet your life."

So the caretaker gave the Man two dollars, and the Man went off and left me.

At first the newness of everything and the unaccustomed smells and getting to know the caretaker, who was a nice old man, prevented my missing the Man, but as the day went on and I began to realize that he had gone and would never come back, I got depressed. I pattered all over the house, whining. It was a most interesting house, bigger than I thought a house could possibly be, but it couldn't cheer me up. You may think it strange that I should pine for the Man, after all the wallopings he had given me, but it is odd, when you come to think of it. But dogs are built like that.

It's a funny thing, but it seems as if it always happened that just when you are feeling most miserable something else happens. As I sat there I heard a motorcycle and somebody shouted.

It was dear old Fred, my old pal Fred, the best old soul that ever stepped! I recognized his voice in a second, and I was scratching at the door before the old man had time to get up out of his chair.

Well, well, well! That was a pleasant surprise! I ran five times round the lawn without stopping, and then I came back and jumped at him.

"What are you doing down here, Fred?" I said. "Is this caretaker your father? How's Mother? I'm living here now. Your father gave two dollars for me. That's twice as much as I was worth when I saw you last."

"Why, it's young Blackie!" That was what they called me at the saloon. "What are you doing here? Where did you get this mutt, Dad?"

"A man sold him to me this morning. Poor old Bob got poisoned. I guess this one ought to be just as good a watchdog. He barks loud enough."

"He should be. His mother is the best watchdog in New York. This cheese-hound used to belong to the boss. Funny, him getting down here."

We went into the house, and had supper. And after supper we sat and talked. Fred was only down for the night, he said, because the boss wanted him back the next day.

"And I'd sooner have my job than yours, Dad," he said. "Of all the lonesome joints! I wonder you aren't scared of burglars."

"I've got my shotgun, and there's the dog. I might be scared if it wasn't for him, but he kind of gives me confidence. Old Bob was the same. Dogs are a comfort in the country."

"Get many tramps here?"

"I've only seen one in two months, and that's the feller who sold me the dog here."

As they were talking about the Man, I asked Fred if he knew him. They might have met at the saloon, when the Man was buying me from the boss.

"You would like him," I said. "I wish you could have met."

The both looked at me.

"What's he growling at?" said Fred. "Think he heard something?"

The old man laughed.

"He wasn't growling. He was talking in his sleep. You're nervous, Fred. It comes from living in the city."

"I guess I am. I like this place in the daytime, but it gives me the willies at night. It's so darned quiet."

His father laughed.

"If you feel that way, Fred, I guess you had best take the gun to bed with you. I shall be quite happy without it."

"You bet I will," said Fred. "I'll take six if you've got them."

And after that they went upstairs. I had a basket in the hall, which had belonged to Bob, the dog who had got poisoned. It was a comfortable basket, but I was so excited at having met Fred again that I couldn't sleep. Besides, there was a smell of mice somewhere and I had to look around for them.

I was just sniffing at a place in the wall, when I heard a scratching noise. At first I thought it was the mice working in a different place, but when I listened I found that the sound came from the window. Somebody was doing something to it from outside.

If it had been Mother, she would have lifted the roof off right there, and so should I, if it hadn't been for what the Man had taught me. I didn't think it possible that this could be the Man come back, for he had gone away and said nothing about ever seeing me again. But I didn't bark. I stopped where I was and listened. And presently the window came open, and somebody began to climb in.

I gave a good sniff, and I knew it was the Man.

I was so delighted that for a moment I nearly forgot myself and shouted with joy, but I remembered in time how shy he was, and stopped myself. But I ran to him and jumped up quite quietly, and he told me to lie down. I was disappointed that he didn't seem more pleased to see me. I lay down.

It was very dark, but he had brought his lantern with him, and I could see him moving about the room, picking things up and putting them in a bag which he had brought with him. Every now and then he would stop and listen, and then he would start moving round again. He was very quick about it, but very quiet. It was plain that he didn't want Fred or his father to come down and find him.

I kept thinking about this peculiarity of his, while I watched him. I suppose, being a mixer myself, I find it hard to understand that everybody else in the world isn't a mixer too. Of course, my experience at the saloon had taught me that men are just as different from each other as dogs. If I chewed Master's shoe, for instance, he used to kick me; but if I chewed Fred's, Fred would tickle me under the ear. And, similarly, some men are shy, and some men are mixers. I quite appreciated that, but I couldn't help feeling that the Man carried shyness to a point where it became morbid. And he didn't give himself a chance to cure himself of it. That was the point. Imagine a man hating to meet people so much that he never visited their houses till the middle of the night, when they were in bed and asleep. It was silly.

As I sat and watched the Man creep about the room it

came to me that here was a chance of doing him a real good turn in spite of himself. Fred was upstairs, and Fred, as I knew by experience, was the easiest man to get along with in the world. Nobody could be shy with Fred. I felt that, if only I could bring him and the Man together, they would get along splendidly, and it would teach the Man not to be silly and avoid people. It would help to give him the confidence which he needed. I had seen him with Bill, and I knew that he could be perfectly natural and easy when he liked.

It was true that the Man might object at first, but after a while he would see that I had acted simply for his good, and would be grateful.

The difficulty was, how to get Fred down without scaring the Man. I knew that if I shouted he wouldn't wait, but would be out of the window and away before Fred could get there. What I had to do was to go to Fred's room, explain the whole situation quietly to him, and ask him to come down and make himself pleasant.

The Man was far too busy to pay any attention to me. He was kneeling in a corner with his back to me, putting something in his bag. I seized the opportunity to steal softly from the room.

Fred's door was shut, and I could hear him snoring. I scratched gently, and then harder, till I heard the snores stop. He got out of bed and opened the door.

"Don't make a noise," I whispered. "Come on down-stairs. I want you to meet a friend of mine."

At first he was quite peevish.

"What's the big idea?" he said, "coming and butting in on a man's beauty-sleep? Get out, you mutt."

He actually started to go back into the room.

"No, on the level, Fred," I said, "I'm not stringing you. There is a man downstairs. He got in through the window. I want you to meet him. He's very shy, and I think it will do him good to have a chat with you."

"What are you whining about?" Fred began, and then he broke off suddenly and listened. We could both hear the Man's footsteps as he moved about.

"Gee!" said Fred softly, and jumped back into the room. He came out, carrying something. He didn't say any more, but started to go downstairs, very quiet, and I went after him.

There was the Man, still putting things in his bag. I was just going to introduce Fred, when Fred, the chump, gave a great yell.

I could have bitten him.

"What did you want to do that for, you big boob?" I said. "I told you he was shy. Now you've scared him."

He certainly had. The Man was out the window quicker than you would have believed possible. He just flew out. I called after him that it was only Fred and me, but at that moment a gun went off with a tremendous bang, so he couldn't have heard me.

I was real angry. The whole thing had gone wrong. Fred seemed to have lost his head entirely. He was behaving like a perfect bonehead. Naturally the Man had been frightened, with him carrying on in that way. I jumped out of the window, to see if I could find the Man and explain, but he was gone. Fred jumped out after me, and nearly squashed me.

I knew the Man could not have gone far, or I should have heard him. I started to sniff around on the chance of picking up his trail. It wasn't long before I struck it.

Fred's father had come down now, and they were running about. The old man had a light. I followed the trail, and it ended at a large cedar tree not far from the house. I stood underneath it and looked up.

"Are you up there?" I shouted. "There's nothing to be scared at. It was only Fred. He's an old pal of mine. He works at the saloon where you bought me. His gun went off by accident. He won't hurt you."

There wasn't a sound. I began to think I must have made a mistake.

"He's got away," I heard Fred say to his father, and just as he said it I caught a faint sound of some one moving in the branches above me.

"No, he hasn't!" I shouted. "He's up this tree."

"I believe the dog's found him, Dad!"

"Yes, he's up here. Come along and get acquainted." Fred came to the foot of the tree.

"You up there," he said, "come along down." Not a sound from the tree.

"It's all right," I explained, "he is up there, but he's very shy. Ask him again."

"All right," said Fred, "stay there if you want to. But I'm going to shoot off this gun into the branches just for fun."

And then the Man started to come down. As soon as he touched the ground, I jumped up at him.

"Great!" I said. "Shake hands with my friend Fred. You'll like him."

But it wasn't any good. They didn't get along together at all. They hardly spoke. The Man went into the house and Fred went after him, carrying his gun. And when they got into the house it was just the same. The Man sat in one chair, and Fred sat in another, and after a long time some men came in an automobile, and the Man went away with them. He didn't say goodby to me.

When he had gone Fred and his father made a great fuss over me. I couldn't understand it. Men are so odd. The Man wasn't a bit pleased that I had brought him and Fred together, but Fred seemed as if he couldn't do enough for me for having introduced him to the Man. However, Fred's father produced some cold ham—my favorite dish—and gave me quite a lot of it, so I stopped worrying over the thing. As Mother used to say, "Don't bother your head about what doesn't concern you. The only thing a dog need concern himself with is the bill-of-fare. Eat your bun, and don't make yourself busy about other people's affairs." In some ways, Mother's was a narrow outlook, but she had a great fund of sterling common sense.

Ulysses and the Dogman

By O. Henry

From *Sixes and Sevens* by O. Henry.
Copyright 1904 by Doubleday.

O. Henry, the pen name of American writer William Sydney Porter, wrote three hundred works of non-fiction, the most famous being "The Gift of the Magi," a story of a young, struggling married couple who each sacrifice something precious in order to give pleasure to the other at Christmas. But for a single twist of fate... ah, but there, as in all his work, O. Henry always listened to the heart. He had seen much of life and believed in common people and honest sentiment. In point of fact, his own story was even more colorful than the ones he wrote.

Young Billy Porter worked at his uncle's drugstore, then went to Texas to be a ranch hand, and subsequently held a job as a bank clerk, which he left to flee to Honduras to avoid charges of embezzlement. Upon returning home to be with his dying wife, he was captured and imprisoned for three years. After he got out, he continued writing until his death. He did not live to see fifty.

"Ulysses and the Dog Man" is one of his lesser known stories, but it packs the same swift punch and a clever twist, which made him famous.

D o you know the time of the Dogman? When the forefinger of twilight begins to smudge the clear drawn lines of the Big City there is inaugurated an hour devoted to one of the most melancholy sights of urban life.

Out from the towering flat crags and apartment peaks of the cliff dwellers of New York steals an army of beings that were once men. Even yet they go upright upon two limbs and retain human forms and speech; but you will observe that they are behind animals in progress. Each of these beings follows a dog, to which he is fastened by an artificial ligament.

These men are all victims to Circe. Not willingly do they become flunkies to Fido, bell boys to bull terriers, and toddlers after Towzer. Modern Circe, instead of turning them into animals, had kindly left the difference of a six-foot leash between them. Every one of those dogmen has been either cajoled, bribed, or commanded by his particular Circe to take the dear household pet out for an airing.

By their faces and manner you can tell that the dogmen are bound in a hopeless enchantment. Never will there come even a dog-catcher Ulysses to remove the spell.

The faces of some are stonily set. They are past the commiseration, the curiosity, or the jeers of their human beings. Years of matrimony, of continuous compulsory canine constitutionals, have made them callous. They unwind their beasts from lamp posts, or the ensnared legs of profane pedestrians, with the solidity of mandarins manipulating the strings of their kites.

Others, more recently reduced to the ranks of Rover's retinue, take their medicine sulkily and fiercely. They play the dog on the end of their line with the pleasure felt by the girl out fishing when she catches a sea-robin on her hook. They glare at you threateningly if you look at them, as if it would be their delight to let slip the dogs of war. These are half-mutinous Dogmen, not quite Circe-ized, and you will do well not to kick their charges, should they sniff at your ankles.

Others of the tribe do not seem to feel so keenly. They are mostly unfresh youths, with gold caps and drooping cigarettes, who do not harmonize with their dogs. The animals they attend wear satin bows in their collars; and the young men steer them so assiduously that you are tempted to the theory that some personal advantage, contingent upon satisfactory service, waits upon the execution of their duties.

The dogs thus personally conducted are of many varieties; but they are one in fatness, in pampered, diseased vileness of temper, in insolent, snarling capriciousness of behaviour. They tug at the leash fractiously, they make leisurely nasal inventory of every door step, railing and post. They sit down to rest when they choose; they wheeze like the winner of a Third Avenue beeksteak-eating contest; they blunder clumsily into open cellars and coal holes; they lead the Dogmen a merry dance.

These unfortunate dry nurses of dogdom, the cur cuddlers, mongrel managers, Spitz stalkers, poodle pullers, Skye scrapers, dachshund dandlers, terrier trailers and Pomeranian pushers of the cliff-dwelling Circes follow their charges meekly. The doggies neither fear nor respect them. Master of the house these men whom they hold in leash may be, but they are not masters of them. From cosy corner to fire escape, from divan to dumb-waiter, doggy's snarl easily drives this two-legged being who is commissioned to walk at the other end of his string during his outing.

One twilight the Dogmen came forth as usual at their Circe's pleading or crack of the whip. One among them was a strong man, apparently of too solid virtues for this airy vocation. His expression was melancholic, his manner depressed. He was leashed to a vile white dog, loathsomely fat, foolishly ill-natured, gloatingly intractable toward his despised conductor.

At a corner nearest to his apartment house the Dogman turned down a side street, hoping for fewer witnesses to his ignominy. The surfeited beast waddled before him, panting with spleen and the labor of motion.

Suddenly the dog stopped. A tall, loud-coated, wide-brimmed man stood like a Colossus blocking the sidewalk and declaring:

"Well, I'm a son of a gun!"

"Jim Berry!" breathed the Dogman, with exclamation points in his voice.

"Sam Telfair," cried Wide-Brim again, "you ding-blasted old willy-walloo, give us your hoof!"

Their hands clasped in the brief, tight greeting of the West that is death to the hand-shake microbe.

"You old fat rascal!" continued Wide-Brim with a wrinkled brown smile, "it's been five years since I seen you. I been in this town a week, but you can't find nobody in such a place. Well, you dinged old married man, how are they coming?"

Something mushy and heavily soft like raised dough leaned against Jim's leg and chewed his leg with a yeasty growl.

"Get to work," said Jim, "and explain this yard-wide

hydrophobic yearling you've throwed your lasso over. Are you the pound-master of this burg? Do you call that a dog or what?"

"I need a drink," said the Dogman, dejected at the reminder of this old dog of the sea. "Come on."

Hard by was a café. 'Tis ever so in the big city.

They sat at a table, and the bloated monster yelped and scrambled at the end of his leash to get at the café cat.

"Whisky," said Jim to the waiter.

"Make it two," said the Dogman.

"You're fatter," said Jim, "and you look subjugated. I don't know about the East agreeing with you. All the boys asked me to hunt you up when I started. Sandy King, he went to the Klondike. Watson Burrel, he married the oldest Peters girl. I made some money buying beeves, and I bought a lot of land upon the Little Powder. Going to fence next fall. Bill Rawlins, he's gone to farming. You remember Bill, of course—he was courting Marcella— excuse me, Sam, I mean the lady you married, while she was teaching school at Prairie View. But you was the lucky man. How is Missis Telfair?"

"S-h-h-h!" said the Dogman, signalling the waiter, "give it a name."

"Whisky," said Jim.

"Make it two," said the Dogman.

"She's well," he continued after his chaser. "She refused to live anywhere but in New York, where she came from. We live in a flat. Every evening at six I take that dog out for a walk. It's Marcella's pet. There never were two animals on earth, Jim, that hated one another like me and that dog does. If you're going to be in the city for a while we will..."

"No, sir-ee. I'm starting for home this evening on the 7:25. Like to stay longer, but I can't."

"I'll walk down to the ferry with you," said the Dogman.

The dog had bound each leg of Jim and the chair together, and had sunk into a comatose slumber. Jim stumbled, and the leash was slightly wrenched. The shrieks of the awakened beast rang for a block around.

"If that's your dog," said Jim when they were on the street again, "what's to hinder you from running that habeas corpus you've got around his neck over a limb and walking off and forgetting him?"

"I'd never dare to," said the Dogman, awed at the bold proposition. "He sleeps in the bed. I sleep on a lounge. He runs howling to Marcella if I look at him. Some night, Jim, I'm going to get even with that dog. I'm going to creep over with a knife and cut a hole in his mosquito bar so they can get in to him. See if I don't do it!"

"You ain't yourself, Sam Telfair. You ain't what you was once. I don't know about these cities and flats over here. With my own eyes I seen you stand off both the Tillotson boys in Prairie View with the brass faucet of a molasses barrel. And I seen you rope and tie the wildest steer on Little Powder in '39, 1-2."

"I did, didn't I?" said the other, with a temporary gleam in his eye. "But that was before I was dogmatized."

"Does Missis Telfair…" began Jim.

"Hush!" said the Dogman. "Here's another café."

They lined up at the bar. The dog fell asleep at their feet.

"Whisky," said Jim.

"Make it two," said the Dogman.

"I thought about you," said Jim, "when I bought that wild land. I wished you was out there to help me with the stock."

"Last Tuesday," said the Dogman, "he bit me on the ankle because I asked for cream in my coffee. He always gets the cream."

"You'd like Prairie View now," said Jim. "The boys from the round-ups for fifty miles ride in there. One corner of my pasture is in sixteen miles of the town. There's a straight forty miles of wire on one side of it."

"You pass through the kitchen to get to the bedroom," said the Dogman, "and you pass through the parlor to get to the bathroom, and you back out of the dining room to get into the bedroom so you can turn around and leave by the kitchen. And he snores and barks in his sleep, and I have to smoke in the park on account of his asthma."

"Don't Missis Telfair…" began Jim.

"Oh, shut up!" said the Dogman. "What is it this time?"

"Whisky," said Jim.

"Make it two," said the Dogman.

"Well, I'll be raking along down to the ferry," said the other.

"Come on there, you mangy, turtle-backed, snake-headed, bench-legged ton-and-a-half of soap grease!" shouted the Dogman, with a new note in his voice and a new hand on the leash. The dog scrambled after them, with an angry whine at such unusual language from his guardian.

At the foot of Twenty-third Street the Dogman led the way through swinging doors.

"Last chance," said he. "Speak up."

"Whisky," said Jim.

"Make it two," said the Dogman.

"I don't know," said the ranchman, "where I'll find the man I want to take charge of the Little Powder outfit. I want somebody I know something about. Finest stretch of prairie and timber you ever squinted your eye over, Sam. Now if you want..."

"Speaking of hydrophobia," said the Dogman, "the other night he chewed a piece out of my leg because I knocked a fly off Marcella's arm. 'It ought to be cauterized,' says Marcella, and I was thinking so myself. I telephones for the doctor, and when he comes, Marcella says to me: 'Help me hold the poor dear while the doctor fixes his mouth. Oh, I hope he got no virus on any of his toofies when he bit you.' Now what do you think of that?"

"Does Missis Telfair..." began Jim.

"Oh, drop it!" said the Dogman. "Come again!"

"Whisky," said Jim.

"Make it two," said the Dogman.

They walked to the ferry. The ranchman stepped to the ticket window.

"Ticket to Denver," said Jim.

"Make it two," said the ex-Dogman.

Buffalo Hunt

By J.A. Hunter

from *Hunter,* by J.A. Hunter.
Harper & Brothers Publishers, New York, 1952.

Born in 1887 in Shearington in the south of Scotland, John Hunter was sent to Africa at the tender age of 18 after it became known that he had shared his affections a little too generously with an older woman who lived in the locality and who happened to be married. His father bought him a half-interest in a farm in Kenya, outside Nairobi and sent him off with his beloved Purdey shotgun to show that despite his son's indiscretions, he was and always would be as beloved to him as his London gun. Once there, he fell heartily into hunting, the sport of his childhood, and met the likes of American hunter Leslie Simpson and "Karamojo" Bell, one of the greatest African hunters best known for hunting elephants with a small-bore rifle.

Hunter decided that farming was not his bailiwick, and began his career as a professional hunter by shooting lions for their hides. It was dangerous business but paid well, at a pound per lion hide and two pounds for leopard. However, after a time, he fell in with the Kenya Game Department and for the rest of his life served the department as a control officer. It was his job to keep the populations of wild game animals in check and to rid the vicinity of dangerous ones. This practice first occurred in Africa shortly after World War I, and it is because of the efforts of people like John Hunter that the conservation of African game animals has been ensured to this very day. It was, at the very least, a dangerous job. As a control officer, Hunter had to deal with vicious beasts, many of whom were man-eaters. It took a formidable man with an iron nerve to spend a lifetime at such work. It takes an even greater man to admit to losing his heart to a much loved dog, as you will see in "Buffalo Hunt."

When Hilda and I returned from Fumve, there was a note awaiting me from Captain Ritchie of the Kenya Game Department. I went to see him at once. The department was confronted by another control problem. In the vicinity of Thomson's Falls, a community some hundred miles north of Nairobi, a herd of buffalo had been doing great damage. The animals were destroying shambas and had killed several natives. Captain Ritchie had come to the conclusion that this herd must be dealt with.

In ordering these animals killed, Captain Ritchie was also interested in the general welfare of all the Kenya buffalo. This particular herd had become a nuisance and Captain Ritchie, ever out to assist the farming community, wanted their numbers kept in check.

Many hunters believe that the buffalo is Africa's most dangerous animal. When a buffalo attacks, he charges with admirable ferocity and will not flinch away from a bullet as do rhinos and even elephants. A buffalo usually continues to charge until he is killed or he has killed the hunter. They are most cunning. Frequently a wounded buffalo will double back and wait beside his trail, hoping to ambush the hunter. Then, too, a buffalo will often attack without any provocation at all, so he may well be regarded as a difficult and uncertain quarry.

I decided to use a heavy rifle on this trip, a .500 double Jeffery. I consider the heaviest weapon a man can conveniently carry is none too powerful for buffalo. Knowing that some of the wounded animals would escape into the bush and have to be driven out, I decided to use dogs. If this appears non-sporting, I can only say I was performing a task assigned to me by the department and I was not interested in personal glory.

The pound in Nairobi contained nothing but a small collection of worthless curs. Still, I was in no position to pick and choose, so I bought the lot. Later, I was able to add to this pack by buying a few larger and more alert dogs from settlers. I still badly needed a "head" dog, a leader of the pack, that would show his mates the way by his courage and determination. Dogs easily follow a leader and even one first-class dog can transform a group of curs into a reasonably respectable pack. No leader was forthcoming so I prepared to leave Nairobi with my mixed bunch of mongrels.

A few days before I left, I received a call from a prominent official asking me to get rid of his pet dog. This animal was considered to be incurably vicious. He had attacked and bitten several natives and was killing livestock near Nairobi. From the owner's description, I decided the dog was hopeless but at that moment anything was grist that came to my mill. I went over to collect him.

At first look, I liked the dog. He was big-boned, tawny in color, and about the size of an Alsatian. He had powerful jaws and clearly knew how to use them. He seemed to be a general crossbreed with a strong dash of bull terrier. I decided to call him Buff, an easy word for the tongue. He took to the name and I felt that we were going to get along well together. I believed him to be a keen, adventuresome animal, never intended by nature to be a house pet. He could not endure being confined in a city, and I knew that feeling well myself. If Buff had lost his temper and chewed up a few bad characters, well, I was not the man to hold that against him.

Buff soon established himself as leader of my pack. There were several that fought him, but they quickly learned discretion. Even the bitches showed preference by transferring their affections to him while the other dogs slunk about at a safe distance. Yet for all his ferocity, Buff was a true dog and would lie at my feet by the hour, looking up at me with his profound, wistful eyes, trying to read my thoughts. Even before we left Nairobi, I was more attached to Buff than I had ever been to any other dog. I could only hope he would prove himself in the buffalo hunts and learn to avoid the fierce animals' horns and sharp hooves.

Near Thomson's Falls I began to realize why Buff's former owner had been so eager to part with him. I took the pack for a stroll one evening and on the way we passed a herd of sheep being driven by a native. The sight of the sheep was too much for Buff. He charged into the flock, cut out a fat-tailed ram, and in a matter of seconds the sheep was on its back with Buff's teeth buried deep in the throat. I tore him off and, removing my belt, gave the dog a beating that he never forgot. Buff took the punishment without a whimper and we returned to camp, Buff cheerfully trotting by my heels all the way.

I had several Nderobo scouts attached to my control camp, a people one-quarter Masai and three-quarters bushman. They are a praiseworthy tribe, being reasonably good hunters, although they do some tilling. We had been at the village only a few hours when I heard a dreadful commotion outside my tent. Rushing out, I found that Buff had knocked down a native woman and was busy disrobing her. Her clothing was only a loin cloth, but he had torn this off and fastened his teeth in her flank. I grabbed Buff by the tail, and exerting all my strength, managed to pull him off. The woman fled for the nearest hut, red and white marks showing on her plump black posterior. I expected a fearful protest from the natives, but the woman's husband was rolling on the ground shouting with laughter and the other natives were equally amused. Several of them came up and congratulated me on having such a fine animal. They considered Buff's aggressiveness a good omen for a buffalo dog.

I talked to the Nderobo concerning the buffalo and heard many stories of the animals' vindictiveness. I quote one of these stories to give the reader some idea of the determination with which a buffalo will follow his victims.

One of the Nderobo walked with a limp and I inquired the cause. The man showed me that his heel was gone—bitten clean off at the ankle. He told me that a buffalo had done it. I could hardly believe this statement, but when he had finished the story, I concluded that the man was telling the truth.

He had been walking through the bush on his way to his shamba, when he heard a snort from the underbrush. He turned and bolted; the thunder of hooves behind told him that his pursuer was a buffalo. The man had a fair start but the buffalo rapidly gained on him. The sound of the hooves grew steadily louder. At the last instant, the man made a desperate jump and managed to grab the limb of a tree just as the buffalo rushed under him. The animal turned and coming back stood below the man, pawing the ground and snorting with fury. The native had pulled his feet up under him but the strain of holding them there grew too much. His right leg became cramped and for a moment he had to extend it. Immediately the waiting buffalo rushed up and nipped off the man's heel with his teeth as though it were a twig. Then, seemingly appeased by the taste of blood he went away, leaving the half-fainting man still clinging to the tree limb.

After thinking the story over, I saw nothing incredible in it. There is no reason why a buffalo should not use his teeth. A horse can give a vicious bite. Indeed, an angry stallion will fight with his teeth quite as much as with his hooves. Later, I was to discover that a buffalo will indeed use his teeth to tear his victims—and very deadly weapons they are. The injuries produced by an infuriated buffalo are often extremely grisly.

The buffalo herd I was after lived in the Marmanet Forest. The cover here is very dense, making hunting both difficult and dangerous. I do not consider a buffalo a formidable animal in the open, but in underbrush he can be very deadly indeed. I was glad I had my dogs with Buff at their head.

I let the pack rest a few days after their trip from Nairobi, then I started out early one morning with my pack and the game scouts. There were buffalo signs throughout the forest and the dogs showed little hesitation in following the tracks. My former pack in the Masai Reserve had been most reluctant to trail lion—the odor of the big cats seemed to daunt them—but apparently dogs are not fearful of buffalo scent. In a few minutes we could hear the buffaloes crashing through the bush with the dogs yelling on their heels. Followed by my native scouts, I kept as close to the pack as I could. Suddenly there came a shrill yelp and I saw one of the dogs go flying up above the bush as a buffalo tossed him. I could not see where he landed. Not wishing to lose dogs unnecessarily, I tried to call them back but in the hubbub of barking I could hardly hear my own voice.

When we came up with the pack, I found they were holding five buffalo bulls at bay. The bulls stood in a ring with their tails together and their horns point outward to keep off the dogs. Suddenly Buff rushed straight for the bunch and grabbed one of the bulls by the nose. The bull plunged forward and tried to dash the dog against the bole of a tree. Buff was not to be squashed so easily and skewed his hindquarters around at the last instant. A bullet from my gun put an end to the bull's struggles.

From then on, Buff always used the same tactics. After the pack had bayed a buffalo cow or bull, Buff would barge in and grab the animal by the nose. When attacked by dogs, buffaloes naturally hold their heads close to the ground to give their horns full play and this habit gave plucky Buff ample opportunity for his favorite hold. Apparently all cattle have tender noses. I remember how in Scotland farmers would put a ring through the nose of a dangerous bull, and as long as the man held the ring, the bull was comparatively helpless. Once Buff got his grip, the buffalo was seldom able to shake him off. Buff took a good stance with all four legs spread wide apart and a buffalo could not get sufficient purchase with his head held down to toss him.

A big buffalo is a grand creature, weighing up to two thousand pounds, with great sweeping ink-black horns as thick as a man's leg at the boss and tapering to points as fine as daggers. When a bull charges with lowered head, he presents his thick skull to you, reinforced by the heavy boss. Under such conditions, only the heaviest caliber rifle can bring him down. In hunting buffalo, I prefer to shoot for the chest, neck, shoulder or under the eye, but in case of a charge you have little choice and must fire where you can.

The dogs were more effective in buffalo hunting than my other pack had been with lions. Dogs can keep out of a buffalo's way more easily than they can avoid a lion's rush. As with my former pack, some of the dogs had more courage than discretion. Instead of dodging an infuriated buffalo's charge, they would stand their ground. A buffalo is so quick in dealing a wipe with either horn or hooves that unless a dog takes good care to leap clear, he will be instantly killed.

Several of the dogs were tossed on different occasions. As a dog went up in the air, the buffalo would watch to see where he was coming down and then make for the spot, hoping to catch the dog while he was still dazed from the fall. The pack would rush in to help their friend, nipping at the buffalo's hocks as I have seen dogs do with domestic cattle, and try to turn him. If they could hold the beast even a moment I was generally able to get a shot.

Even when we encountered a herd of buffalo in the open, I had great trouble getting close enough to them for a shot. Their excellent eyesight and hearing made it hard to approach them. Often I had to whistle on the dogs. The pack would chase the buffalo into the cover and then out again while I fired at the animals almost as though at target practice.

In cover, it was a different matter. A hunted buffalo is wise enough to stand motionless in deep but until the man is almost up to him before starting his charge. Even shooting nearby will not make him move until he is certain of getting his enemy. Here dogs are invaluable. The dogs can often smell the waiting buffalo and give the alarm. If not, they are fairly certain to come on him while they are trotting ahead of the hunter. I have no hesitation in saying that the dogs saved my life a dozen times during these hunts.

Buff was invaluable. He was that rare combination, seldom found among either dogs or humans, of great courage mingled with intelligent discretion. He knew enough to avoid a buffalo's rush and yet had absolutely no fear of the animal. Only when one unusual situation arose was the gallant dog in any real danger.

On one occasion, the pack had taken off after a very large buffalo bull. To keep the dogs from closing with him, the bull had taken up his stand in the center of a stream. This is a common trick among hunted animals when pursued by dogs. The dogs lined up on the river bank, making a great din with their barking, but not caring to swim out to the bull. No so Buff. When he came up, the plucky dog took a great leap into the water and sure enough, managed to grab the surprised bull by the nose. For a moment the old buffalo stood there astonished by such audacity but he quickly recovered from his surprise and countered by pushing Buff under water. Buff would have drowned in a few minutes had I not been able to end the unequal struggle with a bullet. When Buff swam back to shore, coughing and spitting up water, I discovered that he had taken such a fierce grip on the tough gristle of the bull's nose that the tips of his front teeth were broken off. This will give some idea of Buff's strength and determination.

Up to date, this was Buff's seventeenth kill, all the buffalo having been griped and held until I dispatched them.

In the next scrap with a buffalo herd, Buff did not get off scot-free. The pack had surrounded a herd and were holding them together by barking and making quick, heel-nipping rushes. Buff tore in and grabbed a large buffalo cow by her nose. He was holding her but her half-grown calf came to her help and butted the dog in the side with its short, stubby horns. Buff gasped, but refused to release his grip. He would have been killed if my scouts had not shot the two buffalo.

After this misadventure, I retired Buff from hunting until his wounds healed. I had shot over two hundred buffalo and the task of wiping out the herds was almost completed. Buff moped in his enforced security, watching wistfully while the rest of the pack trotted out after me for the day's hunt. One of my scouts went daily to a nearby kraal to get milk for the pack, and I told him to take Buff along on these walks. I felt the exercise would keep Buff from getting stiff while he was recuperating and also give him something to do.

On one of these trips, a warthog crossed Buff's path. This was a familiarity he could not stand. In spite of the shouts of the scout, Buff started all out after him. The hog went down a hole, first turning himself around and backing in so he would have his tusks toward the entrance in true warthog style. Buff was about to go down the hole after him when the hog suddenly charged out. I firmly believe that if Buff had not broken off the points of his teeth, he would have succeeded in holding the animal. Instead, he lost his grip on the pig's sweaty hide. Instantly, the boar made a quick lunge with his tusks and caught Buff in the chest, ripping the brave dog open and killing him instantly. The scout shot the boar but the damage was done. When I returned from my day's hunt, there was the body of my noble Buff, killed at a time when I thought nothing could happen to him.

I have never owned another dog like Buff, before or

since. The rest of the hunt was poisoned for me because of the loss of this great animal. I hoped some of Buff's puppies would take after him, but none of them were fit to run in the same pack with their father. You get too fond of a dog. Not until after his death do you realize how much he meant to you. I sometimes wonder if the pleasure in owning a dog is worth the misery caused by his death.

Verdun Belle

By *Alexander Woollcott*

From *Two Gentlemen and a Lady* by Alexander Woollcott.
Copyright 1928. Permission of Coward-McCann, Inc.

Another member of the Algonquin Round Table was Alexander Woollcott, arguably the most virulent columnist of his day. James Thurber called him as "old Vitriol and Violets, a man as fragile as nails and as sweet as death." Playwrights Kaufman and Hart lampooned him by creating an acidic, pompous portrait of Woollcott as "The Man Who Came to Dinner," which was made into a movie after its popular Broadway run. Novelist Edna Ferber labeled him "that New Jersey Nero, wearing his pinafore like a toga and fiddling while Rome burns."

Corey Ford was "sitting in the Men's Bar at the Ritz when Woollcott paused beside our table, fixed me with his glittering eye, and announced, 'Ford, I plan to spend three days at your house in New Hampshire next week.' The prospect of entertaining such a demanding guest in my modest home was terrifying, but I managed to stammer out a weak 'Gee, Aleck, that will be swell.' 'I'll be the judge of that,' Woollcott retorted, and swept toward the door."

So, for a man like Alexander Woollcott to write "Verdun Belle," a sensitive story about a Brittany spaniel who adopts a corp of American troops in France during World War I, is a puzzlement. What? It took a dog to soften his cynic's heart? Yeah—it did.

I first heard the saga of Verdun Belle one June afternoon under a drowsy apple tree in the troubled valley of the Marne. The story began in a chill, grimy Lorraine village, where, in hovels and haymows, a disconsolate detachment of United States Marines lay waiting the order to go up into the maze of trenches around the citadel bearing the immortal name of Verdun.

Into this village at dusk one day in the early spring of 1918 there came out of space a shabby, lonesome dog—a squat setter of indiscreet, complex and questionable ancestry. One watching her as she trotted intently along the aromatic village street would have sworn that she had an important engagement with the mayor and was, regretfully, a little late.

At the end of the street she came to where a young buck private lounged glumly on a doorstep. Halting in her tracks, she sat down to contemplate him, then, satisfied seemingly by what she sensed and saw, she came over and flopped down beside him in a most companionable manner. His pleased hand reached over and played with one silken chocolate-colored ear.

Somehow that gesture sealed a compact between those two. There was thereafter no doubt in either's mind that they belonged to each other for better or for worse, in sickness and in health, through weal and woe, world without end. She ate when and what he ate. She slept beside him, her muzzle resting on his leg.

To the uninitiated onlookers her enthusiasm may not have been immediately explicable. In the eyes of his top sergeant and his company clerk he may well have seemed an undistinguished warrior. Verdun Belle thought him the most charming person in all the world. There was a loose popular notion that she had joined up with the company as mascot and belonged to them all. She affably let them think so, but she had her own ideas on the subject.

When they moved up into the line she went along and was so obviously trench-broken that they guessed she had already served a hitch with some French regiment in that once desperate region.

In May, when the outfit was engaged in the exhausting activities which the High Command was pleased to describe as "resting," Belle thought it a convenient time to present an interested but amply forewarned regiment with seven wriggling casuals, some black and white, some splotched with the same brown as her own. These newcomers complicated the domestic economy of the leathernecks' haymow, but they did not become an acute problem until that memorable night late in the month when breathless word bade these troops to be up and away.

The Second Division of the A.E.F. was always being thus picked up and flung across France. This time the enemy had snapped up Soissons and Rheims and was pushing with dreadful ease and speed toward the Marne. Ahead of the Marines as they scrambled across the monotonous plain of the Champagne, there lay amid the ripening wheat fields a mean and hilly patch of timber called Belleau Wood. Verdun Belle went along.

The leatherneck solved the problem of the puppies by drowning four and placing the other three in a basket he had begged from a village woman. By night and by day the troop movement was made, now in the wheezing trains, now in swarming lorries, now afoot. Sometimes Belle's crony rode. Sometimes (under pressure of popular clamor against the room he was taking up) he would yield his place to the basket and jog along with his hand on the tailboard, with Belle trotting behind him.

Everyone had assured the stubborn youngster that he would not be able to manage, and now misgivings settled on him like crows. He guessed that Verdun Belle must be wondering too. He turned to assure her that everything would be all right. She was not there. No one within call had seen her quit the line. He kept telling himself she would show up. But the day went and the night came without her.

He jettisoned the basket and pouched the pups in his forest green shirt in the manner of kangaroos. In the morning one of the three was dead. And the problem of transporting the other two was now tangled by the circumstances that he had to feed them.

An immensely interested old woman in the village where they halted at sunup volunteered some milk for the cup of his mess kit, and with much jeering advice from all sides, and, by dint of an eye-dropper from his pack, he tried sheepishly to be a mother to the two waifs. The attempt was not shiningly successful.

As the order was shouted to fall in, he hitched his pack to his back and stuffed his charges back into his shirt. Now, in the morning light, the highway was choked. The battle was close at hand now. Field hospitals, jostling in the river of traffic, sought space to pitch their tents. The top sergeant of one such outfit was riding on the driver's seat of an ambulance. Marines in endless number were moving up fast. It was one of these who, in a moment's halt, fell out of line, leaped to the step of the blockaded ambulance, and looked eagerly into the medico top sergeant's eyes.

"Say, buddy," whispered the youngster, "take care of these for me. I lost their mother in the jam."

The Top found his hands closing on two drowsy pups.

All that day the field hospital personnel was harried by the task of providing nourishment for the two casuals thus unexpectedly attached to them for rations. The Top went over the possible provender and found that the pups were not yet equal to a diet of bread, corn syrup and corned willy.

The problem was still unsolved at sundown, and the pups lay faint in their bed of absorbent cotton, when, bringing up the rear of a detachment of Marines that struggled past, there trotted a brown-and-white setter.

"It would be swell if she had milk in her," the top sergeant said, wondering how he could salvage the mascot of an outfit on the march.

But his larcenous thoughts were waste. She halted dead in her tracks, flung her head high to sniff the air, wheeled sharp to the left and became just a streak of brown and white against the ground. The entire staff formed a jostling circle to watch the family reunion.

After that it was tacitly assumed that these casuals belonged. When the hospital was ordered to shift further back beyond the reach of the whining shells, Verdun Belle and the pups were entrusted to an ambulance driver and went along in style. They all moved—bag, baggage and livestock—into the deserted little Chateau of the Guardian Angel. Operating tables, with acetylene torches to light them, were set up in what had been a tool shed. Cots were strewn in the orchard alongside. Thereafter for a month there was never rest in the hospital.

Surgeons and orderlies spelled each other at times,

snatching morsels of sleep and returned a few hours later to relieve the others. But Verdun Belle took no time off. Between cat naps in the corner, due attentions to her restive brood and an occasional snack for herself, she managed somehow to be on hand for every ambulance, cursorily examining each casualty as he was lifted to the ground.

Then, in the four o'clock of one morning, the orderly bending over a stretcher that had just been rested on the ground was hit by something that half bowled him over.

The projectile was Verdun Belle. Every quivering inch of her proclaimed to all concerned that here was a case she was personally in charge of. From nose to tail tip she was taut with excitement, and a kind of eager whimpering bubbled up out of her. For here was this mess of a leatherneck of hers to be washed up. So like him to get all dirty the moment her back was turned! The first thing he knew as he came to was the feel of a pink tongue cleaning his ears.

I hope there was something prophetic in the closing of the account of Verdun Belle which appeared the next week in the A.E.F. Newspaper, *The Stars and Stripes:* "Before long they would have to ship him on to the evacuation hospital, on from there to the base hospital, on and on. It was not very clear to anyone how another separation could be prevented, but they knew in their hearts they could safely leave the answer to someone else. They could leave it to Verdun Belle."

Some Dogs

By E.C. Keith

From his book, *Gun for Company,* published by Country Life Ltd., London, and Charles Scribner's Sons, New York, 1937.

Who was E.C. Keith, author of Gun for Company? *I wish I knew. Only 175 copies of his book were published, and I cherish mine, No. 37. His last chapter, "Some Dogs," reveals an enthusiastic wingshooter with a deep and abiding love for Labs, and paints a captivating portrait of a solid sportsman and seasoned member of the shooting fraternity. Do not mistake him for American hunter and gun enthusiast Elmer Keith. I garner this Keith wrote* Gun for Company *in his twilight years, because he speaks broadly of shooting in a manner associated with someone who pursued a lifetime afield. I assume he was a soldier in the First World War, and reckon he saw too clearly, in 1937 (when his book was published, in London), a horizon darkened with the threat of a second world war. Perhaps he was anxious to pen his memories before the world again was torn apart. One thing is clear. World War II closed, arguably, the most colorful chapter in the sport of wingshooting. We try, as best we can, to hold on to its lure. Problem is, we can't catch that fleeting commodity, Time; and when given a dose of leisure, precious few know how to handle it. We lust for a chance to live endless days behind a confidential retriever, and follow him into fields edged with thick hedgerows, plush with coveys; or watch him crash into a waterfowl-splendid lake for a textbook retrieve. The great British institution, the aristocratic "Country Set," is unable to survive this fast-paced world of ours. It, too, is destined to be a pleasant way of life that, alas, must be left behind, and drift graciously into the past.*

Given a sense of humour and the ability to draw, what an amusing book of caricatures one might compile on dogs and dog owners in the shooting field! To convert the many tragedies and ecstasies into comedies would not be difficult for anyone quite detached from the realities.

On the whole, the standard of dog work in the average shooting field is of a very high order, in spite of the peculiar and spasmodic handling to which many dogs are subjected, and which must necessarily produce a wide variation in their methods of working. Quite nine people out of ten think that they are good and competent dog handlers, whereas the gifted few who can consistently improve the working of a young dog and do credit to its intelligence are very much in the minority.

It would be quite safe to say that most shooting men are dog enthusiasts, but that is very different from being good dog men, and by that I mean men who are competent to train and handle a dog and get the best out of it. All like to try and most think they succeed, but the perfect partnership is not often seen; and yet the amount of pleasure derived from having a dog with one and working it on game goes a long way towards making the day enjoyable, and that enjoyment is by no means regulated by the efficiency of the work. A good dog man with a good dog is usually inconspicuous; the two function so quietly and unostentatiously that little notice is attracted. There are no fussing and petting when a bird is brought to hand, and no disturbing shouts and whistles.

On the other hand, the doting owner with a moderate dog—and the two often go together—is so delighted with the most mediocre performance that he is quite oblivious of the distracting commotion which his efforts to control and assist the dog have caused. If, however, one were to suggest tentatively that the qualities of his dog were hardly such as to make it a valuable contribution to the success of the day, he would, quite rightly, be highly indignant. It was a young dog, he would say, and would in time be perfectly brilliant; it only wants work. And so the inferior dog remains young for many years in spite of work and coaxing and beating, but, all the same, the owner derives a great deal of enjoyment from it. That it should suddenly disappear over the skyline and probably be made for a young dog! It is, however, particularly annoying to the man who is trying to run his shoot quietly and efficiently, if his guests insist on making use of this day for the training of their dogs.

Then there is the man who cannot be bothered with a dog; he wants to shoot, and dogs, to him, are a nuisance. Many a suffering host has had cause to wish that all guns were as this man, so that his day might be run in peace and quietude. To admit honestly that the actual shooting is sufficient without the distracting influence of a dog (probably bad) is by no means unsporting, and at the end of the day this man is little the worse off. If he has a lost bird, there are many who will readily respond to his request for assistance, and take it as a compliment to their dog to be asked to work it for another man's bird. If this man could be persuaded that it was the right thing to add a dog to his regular equipment, it would be extremely unlikely that he would have sufficient patience and skill to handle it efficiently.

Between these two extremes there lies a large number of good and well-handled dogs which are a great asset to any shooting day; they and their owners work quite naturally together without any fuss and bother and with no interference with the day's program. It is certainly a very great pleasure to see a good dog carefully ranging over the ground where its master's birds are likely to have fallen, or following up a runner for some considerable distance. The owner is confident that if his dog has gone far afield it is certainly on a runner, and will come straight back when the bird is found or when scent fails. There is no need for him to whistle and shout for fear that it has gone off on a hunting expedition of its own. And any such noise is most distracting to all concerned, and certainly other dogs work less well when this is going on.

But when the wide ranging, uncontrollable animal insists on working the ground behind the whole line, picking up any bird it may chance to come across—that is too annoying for words. However, annoyance of this kind is short-lived, unless of course, it becomes too persistent, but from an onlooker's point of view, there is often a very funny side. It is good to see a man devoted to his dog, and however unworthy that animal may be of a place in the shooting field, its owner probably enjoys having it with him as much as the man with the perfect dog.

There is a wide diversity of opinion on the qualities which constitute the ideal shooting dog, and this must remain so long as there is no definite standard of training, and each man trains according to his own ideas; in this way also there will always be that variation in the working methods of the individual dog. One man may prefer a steady, close working dog which is always under complete control, however much that method may restrict the worker, while another likes more dash and independence.

Certainly it seems to me that the perfect dog should be allowed sufficient liberty in order to exercise its own natural intelligence. One does not require a dog to pick the birds which are obvious and easily gathered, but to search for the difficult ones, the runners, and those which hide as so many wounded birds do.

In this respect, I think that the good, general purpose shooting dog is infinitely superior to the field-trial worker which rarely retrieves a bird other than that which anyone might walk out and gather. I never attend a field trial without thinking how much better and more interesting is the work one may see with the average shooting party where the dogs have more freedom and therefore develop more enterprise. My complaint is that the field-trial dog is not taught to use its head, but rather to heed carefully the instructions of the worker, and therefore too much of its attention to monopolized in this way; but this, I think, is the case with all show dogs; they become devoid of the common sense and intelligence which characterize the ideal dog, whether it be a gun dog or merely a companion.

I used to think that good gun dogs were made and not born, but now I am convinced that the reverse is more usual. In a few cases a good man may, with difficulty, convert a naturally inferior dog, but usually the best dogs are born good. There is more in breeding than in training, and the well-bred dog with an instinct for work requires very little rearing.

I had one very convincing proof of this, and here let me admit that I am not a good dog man. I have neither the patience nor the mentality to train dogs, but all the same, I am very fond of them, and to have a good one with me in the shooting field contributes a great deal to my enjoyment. When shooting alone, a dog is more than ever essential. Besides doing a lot of necessary work in acting as a combined beater and retriever, it is a great companion, and one that feels that the dog represents fully half the day's enjoyment. It is on such days that a lasting friendship is cemented; a mutual understanding which is the necessary foundation to a perfect partnership. I have often noticed how much better a dog works when there are no others to attract its attention or interfere with its work; and no doubt it is the same with humans—they have then more time to cooperate with the dog, so that the joint activities run more smoothly. I like to feel that my dog and I are friends; confidential companions with a mutual enjoyment of the sport. But if my dog repeatedly did the wrong thing it would bore me intensely and we should no longer be friends.

In regard to my contention that breeding counts most. I was once given a young and very well-bred Labrador, and knowing my own incapacity for good handling, I gave it to my keeper to train. In less than a fortnight he brought it back, saying that it was a natural worker and required little training. Although this seemed to me to be most unlikely, I gave the dog a trail and soon found that the keeper's view was justified. Susan turned out to be the dog of a lifetime, and I never expect to have another anything like as good. She was the mother of many dogs which all proved to be reasonably good, but there was never another Susan, or one which could hold a candle to her.

Of course, I know that everyone has a dog which is the best ever, but then others have probably been well trained and carefully handled. Susan had no such educational advantages, but we at once became great friends, with an understanding of each other's peculiarities. There was no question of being steady, or ranging wide or of doing anything stupid; Susan was much too sensible. She understood her work for A to Z, and it was the greatest possible pleasure to watch her at it.

In later days I felt that I was the lesser part of the combination and that Susan herself was convinced that she mattered more. She had her peculiarities, of course, but these were not unreasonable. One was that she insisted on seeing what was going on and in taking up a position during a drive from which she could see the birds fall. A favourite one was either on the wall of a grouse butt or in the heather a few yards away; never would she stray inside. It was the same during a snipe drive—nothing would induce her to come inside the butt and remain there. But it did not matter; she never disgraced me nor did the wrong thing, and even if she thought it necessary to retrieve a near-by runner during the drive, it was all done so quietly and quickly that it was hardly noticed. Many a time she has crossed the horizon on a grouse moor, to return perhaps ten minutes later with the bird. I felt no compunction about leaving her to it; even if I walked on to the next line of butts she would follow me there.

After the last drive, Susan had no further use for me. My loader was her feeder, and him she followed; her one great weakness was food. I might call her, but with no effect; shooting was over, and the next thing was supper; she would turn her head and look at me as to say, "You be blowed; I want my food." I always had a feeling that the gun attracted Susan to me just as the food attracted her to her feeder, but if shooting and feeding times should have clashed, I am afraid that food would probably have won the day. This weakness for good living, together with the over-indulgence of her feeder, soon played havoc with Susan's figure, so much so that her many admirers recommended a course of slimming in order to add to her activity and grace; but fat dogs, like fat people, have their advantages they are, as rule, placid and pleasant and companionable. The thin, nervy rake may appear to be more efficient and to cover more ground, but reasoning power goes a long way to counterbalance this. Those people who were the most scathing about Susan's waist-line measurement were the first to respond to the hazel-brown appealing eyes and uplifted black paw with tid-bits from the luncheon table, so this very general vice went on unchecked.

It was by water that Susan really excelled. Of course, she knew every inch of my bog and the river which bounded one side, as well as the habits of the fowl which fell there, and so practice made her perfect. If a wounded duck or teal fell in the reeds near the river I knew that a fascinating contest would follow. Susan was perfectly well aware that the invariable habit of a wounded duck is to make for water, and she should keep an eye on this while hunting the reeds; and then, when she and it were in the water, the final act of the drama was played with patience and with great reasoning. Paddling in mid-stream, Susan would wait for the diver to come to the surface, and if it did not do so within a reasonable time she would return to the bank and hunt the reeds again. The end was always the same—no matter how much patience and perseverance was required Susan eventually got her way.

During an evening duck flight she was the greatest possible assistance. Her pricked ears and expectant manner would tell me that she had heard ducks before I had, and then, after the shot, she would listen for the "plop," and her nose would indicate the direction in which the bird fell; and later, there was no need for me to stagger through mud and water with a torch in a vain attempt to pick up. Susan would quietly and methodically gather those that were at all possible, and if she failed it would certainly be a waste of time for me to try. As a rule, when duck or snipe shooting, she would pick each bird as it fell without any instruction to go out and do so. By marking well, it was all done so quickly and efficiently that the drive or flight suffered not at all; but at a partridge drive the next day she would again be as steady as a rock, recognizing the altered circumstances and the need for patience.

It was on the marsh and the bog, at the evening and morning flights, where we did most of our sporting, that Susan and I got to know each other well and to understand the other's requirements. She was, in my opinion, the ideal gun dog; she gave me no anxiety or worry and in return I left her alone to work as she thought best, for certainly her methods of marking and finding could not have been improved upon. In old age her lack of activity was to some extent made up for by increased intelligence, but before life became a burden to her she met a sad but swift end on the railway.

As an all-round gun dog I do not think there is anything to touch a black Labrador. Their intelligence is so marked, and with it an activity combined with steadiness which I have never found in any other breed. Spaniels are delightful and their keenness is exhilarating, but they rarely remain steady. I have owned several spaniels and have been very fond of them all, but after a few seasons they became more suited to the rough shoot. Of course, on a marsh or other rough ground where hunting is the main work, they are excellent, but for diving—it is anxious work to control a spaniel, and a dog tied down is not much amusement.

My first dog was a spaniel. His pedigree would not bear inspection, but for the work I wanted then there could have been no better. There was no orthodox training; he just happened, and there sprang up between us a partnership on equal terms. We were both beginners, both experimenting in an unknown land where there was so much we were anxious to discover. How he hunted the standing corn to force rabbits across the nibbled-down space by which I was waiting! He would follow close on my heels until I gave him the order to go, when, with a wild rush, he was out into the corn, zig-zagging about until he found his quarry, and then—I could see by the movement of the corn—a mad dash straight for the rabbit sanctuary in the fence. How near my shots often were to his nose I hardly like to think, but if an odd pellet reached him he never complained. Or on the low meadows where clumps of thorn and brambles harboured many a bunny. He would know in an instant if one was at home and then race excitedly round the bush in case it should escape. He trusted my gun not a bit and his one object was to catch the rabbit himself. The word "steadiness" did not exist in his vocabulary, but for showing sport there was no better dog.

Prince was his name, and to me a prince of dogs he was. Rabbits were his strong point; his thoughts and dreams were all of rabbits. Many a time he buried himself digging for one in sandy ground, for he was an all-round sportsman and could turn his hand to any form of the game. I remember him once killing so many rats that he was violently sick, but then he and I took the rough with the smooth in those days and made no fuss about it.

The only dog I ever trained myself was a black cocker spaniel. He was intended to be a pet, but soon showed such remarkable intelligence that I amused myself training him for shooting. I was recovering from an illness at the time and had, of necessity, to be patient. For hours we would play seek and find in the shrubbery, and eventually he understood almost every word I spoke to him. How he enjoyed and looked forward to those lessons!

In no other form of animal life—not excluding the human race—could one find such keenness and sheer joy in an education; nor can any other dog be so devoted and affectionate as a spaniel. It is, in their case, a matter of hero worship; false gods perhaps, but such a devotion is almost pathetic. In due course, Zulu was introduced to the gun and to game. For the first season he was nearly perfect, and in following and retrieving a runner even Susan would not have been disgraced. I believe a spaniel has a better nose than any other breed. Later he developed fits, and for some time I thought he would never recover. I always think that I overworked his brain, and as he was unusually intelligent, it was more than his health could stand. However, after about a year, he recovered and lived to a good old age as a very favourite companion, but no longer as a gun dog; I was afraid the excitement might cause the fits to return, and besides, he became unsteady—hares always proved too much for him; and hares in Norfolk are a dreadful trial and a sore temptation to any dog.

One day I was walking across a field with another gun to line the next fence, when my companion spotted a half-grown hare squatting on its seat. What should he do but stalk it on hands and knees and eventually catch it. I remarked that it was generally supposed that a hare so handled would not live, and to confound my theory this leveret, when released, legged it for all it was worth in the direction of the next drive, a root field. In a moment a black object dashed off in pursuit; I had forgotten that Zulu was behind me and that hares were his one weak point; but it was too late.

I did nothing and said nothing while he raced on a futile errand, now leagues behind his quarry. Would he stop or should I have the mortification of seeing the next drive ruined while he hunted the roots, sending coveys in all directions? Right up to the fence he went and on to the bank, where he hesitated, then, turning to look at me, he trotted off back, wagging his black, curly stump of a tail as much as to say, "I'm not such a fool as you think." Of course, he should have been beaten, but one cannot beat spaniels—they are far too affectionate; and besides, there should be an unalterable rule against beating dogs in the shooting-field. It is hard not to do so at times when they become unreasonably proactive, but it is not a matter in which master and dog are alone concerned; nothing is more unpopular and unpleasant.

There are many breeds of dogs which have great sporting instincts. A dachshund can become quite a good retriever with careful training, but it hardly has what one might describe as a sporting figure. I was once staying in a house where a very sporting dachshund was the apple of his owner's eye, an owner who was exceptionally fond of all dogs, and in whose opinion they could do no wrong. There was a trout stream on the property, and there many otters played havoc with the trout and defied all attempts to reduce their numbers.

One afternoon we went for a walk by the river with the dogs, and incidentally with a gun, but I could not imagine that, however voracious otter might be, one would present an opportunity in broad daylight. However, it was the custom to take a gun on the off chance, so I thought no more about it, and the two dogs—a spaniel and the dachshund—had a right royal time hunting rabbits. We were about to turn for home when the spaniel became greatly excited in one clump of reeds and raced round it in unusual ecstasy. "An otter," exclaimed my friend, and went to the river's edge to intercept it, while I assisted the spaniel.

It was all done in a few moments, and before either of us had time to think. The reeds in the centre were moving gently, an object was slowly but surely making for the river. My friend could see its whereabouts and fired. There was a sharp, pathetic yelp, and then we both realized the terrible tragedy which had been enacted. I had seen a terrier accidentally shot and killed; twice seen a retriever killed on the road by a car; and a favourite dog die from strychnine poison, but none of these tragedies seemed so great as the death of poor Fritz. Had I fired the shot it would have been better, and had I myself been shot it could have caused no more grief.

Some people become so fond of dogs that I really think that there are instances where it would be better not to own one. Their lives are so short and subject to so many risks that the inevitable end causes too much regret;

and an ailing dog is a pathetic patient; he can tell one so little and expects one to be able to do so much. It is a great responsibility to own dogs, to take charge of their lives and to adopt them as slaves, for slaves they are only too willing to be. They are so faithful and affectionate, and ask for no more than to be with their guardian, to share his interests; and a dog which has played an important part in so many enjoyable days, entering into the spirit of the sport and into the science of it, becomes an invaluable treasure. It is only when he becomes prematurely old, as so many gun dogs seem to do, that we can fully appreciate what a delightful companion we have lost. Never has he been moody or ill-tempered, and ever reluctant to join in the game and do his utmost to assist.

A dog never admits that he is cold, or tired, or hungry; then when he is old and probably rheumatic, as all dogs used in water are apt to become, we wonder whether we have always been sufficiently considerate. That cold morning, duck flighting, when he had to stand for an hour in freezing water, while we were comfortably garbed in long boots; and the many nights when he has come home very wet and cold; did we always dry him carefully before attending to our own comforts? Perhaps that is the reason why he is now limping painfully, cramped with rheumatism?

I am probably not alone in realizing that lack of consideration has cost a faithful servant and friend a few years of useful service and enjoyment; but a dog makes no complaints. We may be dissatisfied with him, but he sees no fault in us; he is faithful and constant to the end, whatever treatment may be meted out to him. This is a canine peculiarity—treatment in no way affects a dog's loyalty and the owner who makes a great fuss of him receives no greater service and affection than the one who neglects or even ill-treats him. A dog rarely resents or bears malice, and one kind word as a rule will cause the greatest injustice to be forgiven; but perhaps the treatment which a dog appreciates most is the happy medium—the master who treats him as he would a normal human friend.

With the Cougar Hounds

By Theodore Roosevelt

Excerpted from *Outdoor Pastimes of An American Hunter*
by Theodore Roosevelt.
Copyright 1905 by Charles Scribner's Sons.

In 1893, Theodore Roosevelt wrote Outdoor Pastimes of An American Hunter. *It was one of more than twenty books, countless articles, and a staggering 150,000 letters that he would write during his lifetime.*

By the time Outdoor Pastimes *was published, "Teddy" was the father of a fine family that ultimately would number a half-dozen children, five by his second wife, Edith Kermit Carow. Nine years before, he had lost his first wife, Alice Hathaway Lee, to Bright's Disease—and his mother to typhoid fever—within hours of one another. On that day, too, Roosevelt's first child, Alice Lee, was born. Whether her mother ever held her is not known; that Teddy embraced his beloved wife in his arms until she ceased to breathe is.*

Heartbroken, Roosevelt left his newborn daughter in the trustworthy and affectionate care of his eldest sister, "Bamie," a kindly, childless woman who had married late in life. Declining renomination for a fourth term in the New York Legislature, Roosevelt headed West for the Badlands of South Dakota to start his life all over again, this time as a rancher. He bought a small cattle ranch and spent long, hard days, in and out of the saddle, working his holding. An avid and expert hunter, he went after elk, buffalo, deer, and, as you'll see, cougar.

What follows is the first chapter of Outdoor Pastimes of An American Hunter. *Here the original text has been condensed for the purpose of focusing on the dogs Roosevelt hunter over. It's a keen view of the most famous rough rider of them all, and some rough-riding hounds he hunted with under the most difficult and demanding of conditions.*

Animals were a very important part of the Roosevelt family's life at Sagamore Hill, the home Teddy built in Oyster Bay on Long Island, New York, for his family. The White

House was, for two terms, their residence while Roosevelt served as the 26th President of the United States, from 1901–1909, but the family returned frequently to Sagamore Hill whenever they could during Teddy's presidency. There he kept an excellent stable of horses, and dogs of every size and shape. In fact, dogs were so important at Sagamore Hill that, as one visitor put it, "The house is rotten with dogs."

You'll be struck, in this chapter, with the early appearance of Roosevelt's written observations of the selective hunting of game animals and herd management. From this seed, his commitment to the conservation of America's wildlife and land would grow and bear much fruit. Years later, Roosevelt remarked that he felt his greatest public achievement was his conservation program, which added over 250 million acres to national forests. Today, U.S. National Park Service manages over 46,000 square miles of parkland. "To waste, to destroy, our natural resources, to skin and exhaust the land instead of using it so as to increase its usefulness, will result in undermining in the days of our children the very prosperity which we ought by right to hand down to them amplified and developed," he addressed Congress on December 3, 1907.

On the night of January 6, 1919, while World War I continued to rage in Europe, one of Teddy's sons, Archie, sent telegrams to each of his three brothers, who were fighting in Germany. A soldier, too, Archie had been wounded there, and was home at Sagamore Hill recuperating from his wounds. "The old lion is dead," he wrote, apt words that said it all. But Roosevelt, who was sixty years old, said it best when he spoke his last words "Put out the light." For him, it was time. For a nation, he would become timeless, and a legend who, as Mount Rushmore attests, was one of the greatest Americans who ever lived.

In January, 1901, I started on a five weeks' cougar hunt from Meeker in northwest Colorado. My companions were Mr. Philip B. Stewart and Dr. Gerald Webb, of Colorado Springs; Stewart was the caption of the victorious Yale nine of '86. We reached Meeker on January 11th, after a forty mile drive from the railroad, through the bitter winter weather; it was eighteen degrees below zero when we started. At Meeker we met John B. Goff, the hunter, and left town the next morning on horseback for his ranch, our hunting beginning that same afternoon, when after a brisk run our dogs treed a bobcat. After a fortnight Stewart and Webb returned, Goff and I staying out three weeks longer. We did not have to camp out, thanks to the warm-hearted hospitality of the proprietor and Manager of the Keystone Ranch, and of the Mathes Brothers and Judge Foreman, both of whose ranches I also visited. The five weeks were spent hunting north of the White River, most of the time in the neighborhood of Coyote Basin and Colorado Mountain. In midwinter, hunting on horseback in the Rockies is apt to be cold work, but we were too warmly clad to mind the weather. We wore heavy flannels, jackets lined with sheepskin, caps which drew down entirely over our ears, and on our feet heavy ordinary socks, German socks, and overshoes. Galloping through the brush and among the spikes of the dead cedars meant that now and then one got snagged; I found tough overalls better than trousers; and most of the time I did not need the jacket, wearing my old buckskin shirt, which is to my mind a particularly useful and comfortable garment.

It is a high, dry country, where the winters are usually very cold, but the snow not under ordinary circumstances very deep. It is wild and broken in character, the hills and low mountains rising in sheer slopes, broken by cliffs and riven by deeply cut and gloomy gorges and ravines. The sage-brush grows everywhere upon the flats and hillsides. Large open groves of pinyon and cedar are scattered over the peaks, ridges, and table-lands. Tall spruces cluster in the cold ravines. Cottonwoods grow along the stream courses, and there are occasional patches of scrub-oak and quaking aspen. The entire country is taken up with cattle ranges wherever it is possible to get a sufficient water supply, natural or artificial. Some thirty miles to the east and north the mountains rise higher, the evergreen forest becomes continuous, the snow lies deep all through the winter, and such Northern animals as the wolverine, lucivee, and snow-shoe rabbit are found. This high country is the summer home of the Colorado elk, now woefully diminished in numbers, and of the Colorado blacktail deer, which are still very plentiful, but which, unless better protected, will follow the elk in the next few decades. I am happy to say that there are now signs to show that the State is waking up to the need of protecting both elk and deer; the few remaining mountain sheep in Colorado are so successfully protected that they are said to be increasing in numbers. In winter both elk and deer come down to the lower country, through a part of which I made my hunting trip. We did not come across any elk, but I have never, even in the old days, seen blacktail more abundant than they were in this region. The bucks had not lost their antlers, and were generally, but not always found in small troops by themselves; the does, yearlings, and fawns—now almost yearlings themselves—went in bands. They seemed tame, and we often passed close to them before they took alarm. Of course at that season it was against the law to kill them; and even had this not been so none of our party would have dreamed of molesting them.

Flocks of Alaskan long-spurs and of rosy finches flitted around the ranch buildings; but at that season there was not very much small bird life.

The midwinter mountain landscape was very beautiful, whether under the brilliant blue sky of the day, or the starlight or glorious moonlight of the night, or when under the dying sun the snowy peaks, and the light clouds above, kindled into flame, and sank again to gold and amber and somber purple. After the snow-storms the trees, almost hidden beneath the light, feather masses, gave a new and strange look to the mountains, as if they were giant masses of frosted silver. Even the storms had a beauty of their own. The keen, cold air, the wonderful scenery, and the interest and excitement of the sport made our veins thrill and beat with buoyant life.

In cougar hunting the success of the hunter depends absolutely upon his hounds. As hounds that are not perfectly trained are worse than useless, this means that success depends absolutely upon the man who trains and hunts the hounds. Goff was one of the best hunters with whom I have ever been out, and he had trained his pack to a point of perfection for its special work, which I have never known another such pack to reach. With the exception of one new hound, which he had just purchased, and of a puppy, which was being trained, not one of the pack would look at a deer even when they were all as keen as mustard, were not on a trail, and when the deer got up but fifty yards or so from them. By the end of the hunt both the new hound and the puppy were entirely trustworthy;

of course, Goff can only keep up his pack by continually including new or young dogs with the veterans. As cougar are only plentiful where deer are infinitely more plentiful, the first requisite for a good cougar hound is that it shall leave its natural prey, the deer, entirely alone. Goff's pack ran only bear, cougar, and bobcat. Under no circumstances were they ever permitted to follow elk, deer, antelope, or, of course, rabbit. Nor were they allowed to follow a wolf unless it was wounded; for in such a rough country they would at once run out of sight and hearing, and moreover if they did overtake the wolf they would be so scattered as to come up singly and probably be overcome one after another. Being big dogs they were always especially eager after wolf and coyote, and when they came across the trail of either, though they would not follow it, they would usually challenge loudly. If the circumstances were such that they could overtake the wolf in a body, it could make no effective fight against them, no matter how large and powerful. On the one or two occasions when this had occurred, the pack had throttled "Isegrim" without getting a scratch.

As the dogs did all the work, we naturally became extremely interested in them, and rapidly grew to know the voice, peculiarities, and special abilities of each. There were eight hounds and four fighting dogs. The hounds were of the ordinary Eastern type, used from the Adirondacks to the Mississippi and the Gulf in the chase of deer and fox. Six of them were black and tan and two were mottled. They differed widely in size and voice. The biggest, and, on the whole, the most useful, was Jim, a very fast, powerful, and true dog with a great voice. When the animal was treed or bayed, Jim was especially useful because he never stopped barking; and we could only find the hounds, when at bay, by listening for the sound of their voices. Among the cliffs and precipices the pack usually ran out of sight and hearing if the chase lasted any length of time. Their business was to bring the quarry to bay, or put it up a tree, and then to stay with it and make a noise until the hunters came up. During this hunt there were two or three occasions when they had a cougar up a tree for at least three hours before we arrived, and on several occasions Goff had known them to keep a cougar up a tree overnight and to be still barking around the tree when the hunters at last found them the following morning. Jim always did his share of the killing, being a formidable fighter, though too wary to take hold until one of the professional fighting dogs had seized. He was a great bully with the other dogs, robbing them of their food, and yielding only to Turk. He possessed great endurance, and very stout feet.

On the whole the most useful dog next to Jim was old Boxer. Age had made Boxer slow, and in addition to this, the first cougar we tackled bit him through one hind leg, so that for the remainder of the trip he went on three legs, or, as Goff put it, "packed one leg"; but this seemed not to interfere with his appetite, his endurance, or his desire for the chase. Of all the dogs he was the best to puzzle out a cold trail on a bare hillside, or in any difficult place. He hardly paid any heed to the others, always insisting upon working out the trail for himself, and he never gave up. Of course, the dogs were much more apt to come upon the cold than upon the fresh trail of a cougar, and it was often necessary for them to spend several hours in working out a track which was at least two days old. Both Boxer and Jim had enormous appetites. Boxer was a small dog and Jim a very large one, and as the relations of the pack among themselves were those of brutal wild-beast selfishness, Boxer had to eat very quickly if he expected to get anything when Jim was around. He never ventured to fight Jim, but in deep-toned voice appealed to heaven against the unrighteousness with which he was treated; and time and again such appeal caused me to sally out and rescue his dinner from Jim's highway robbery. Once, when Boxer was given a biscuit, which he tried to bolt whole, Jim simply took his entire head in his jaws, and convinced him that he had his choice of surrendering the biscuit, or sharing its passage down Jim's capacious throat. Boxer promptly gave up the biscuit, then lay on his back and wailed a protest to fate—his voice being deep rather than loud, so that on the trail, when heard at a distance, it sounded a little as if he was croaking. After killing a cougar we usually cut up the carcass and fed it to the dogs, if we did not expect another chase that day. They devoured it eagerly, Boxer, after his meal, always looking as if he had swallowed a mattress.

Next in size to Jim was Tree'em. Tree'em was a good dog, but I never considered him remarkable until his feat on the last day of our hunt, to be afterward related. He was not a very noisy dog, and when "barking treed" he had a meditative way of giving single barks separated by intervals of several seconds, all the time gazing stolidly up at the big, sinister cat which he was baying. Early in the hunt, in the course of a fight with one of the cougars, he received some injury to his tail, which made it hang down like a piece of old rope. Apparently it hurt him a good deal and we let him rest for two weeks. This put him in great spirits and made him fat and strong, but only enabled him to recover power over the root of the tail, while the tip hung down as before; it looked like a curved pump-handle when he tried to carry it erect.

Lil and Nel were two very stanch and fast bitches, the only two dogs that could keep up to Jim in a quick burst. They had shrill voices. Their only failing was a tendency to let the other members of the pack cow them so that they did not get their full share of the food. It was not a pack in which a slow or timid dog had much chance for existence. They would all unite in the chase and the fierce struggle which usually closed it; but the instant the quarry was killed each dog resumed his normal attitude of greedy anger or greedy fear toward the others.

Another bitch rejoiced in the not very appropriate name of Pete. She was our most ardent huntress. In the middle of our trip she gave birth to a litter of puppies, but before they were two weeks old she would slip away after us and join with the utmost ardor in the hunting and fighting. Her brother Jimmie, although of the same age (both were young), was not nearly as far advanced. He would run well on a fresh trail, but a cold trail on a long check always discouraged him and made him come back to Goff. He was rapidly learning; a single beating taught him to let deer alone. The remaining hound, Bruno, had just been added to the pack. He showed tendencies both to muteness and babbling, and at times, if he thought himself unobserved, could not resist making a sprint after a deer; but he occasionally rendered good service. If Jim or Boxer gave tongue every member of the pack ran to the sound; but not a dog paid any heed to Jimmie or Bruno. Yet both ultimately because first-class hounds.

The fighting dogs always trotted at the heels of the

horses, which had become entirely accustomed to them, and made no objection when they literally rubbed against their heels. The fighters never left us until we came to where we could hear the hounds "barking treed," or with their quarry at bay. Then they tore in a straight line to the sound. They were the ones who were expected to do the seizing and take the punishment, though the minute they actually had hold of the cougar, the hounds all piled on too, and did their share of the killing; but the seizers fought the head while the hounds generally took hold behind. All of them, fighters and hounds alike, were exceedingly good-natured and affectionate with their human friends, though short-tempered to a degree with one another. The best of the fighters was old Turk, who was by blood half hound and half "Siberian bloodhound." Both his father and his mother were half-breeds of the same strains, and both were famous fighters. Once, when Goff had wounded an enormous gray wolf in the hind leg, the father had overtaken it and fought it to a standstill. The two dogs together were an overmatch for any wolf. Turk had had a sister who was as good as he was; but she had been killed the year before by a cougar which bit her through the skull; accidents being, of course frequent in the pack, for a big cougar is an even more formidable opponent to dogs than a wolf. Turk's head and body were seamed with scars. He had lost his lower fangs, but he was still a most formidable dog. While we were at the Keystone Ranch a big steer which had been driven in, got on the fight, and the foreman, William Wilson, took Turk out to aid him. At first Turk did not grasp what was expected of him, because all the dogs were trained never to touch anything domestic—at the different ranches where we stopped the cats and kittens wandered about, perfectly safe, in the midst of this hard-biting crew of bear and cougar fighters. But when Turk at last realized that he was expected to seize the steer, he did the business with speed and thoroughness; he not only threw the steer, but would have killed it then and there had he not been, with much difficulty, taken away. Three dogs like Turk, in their prime and with their teeth intact, could, I believe, kill an ordinary female cougar, and could hold even a big male so as to allow it to be killed with the knife.

Next to Turk were two half-breeds between bull and shepherd, named Tony and Baldy. They were exceedingly game, knowing-looking little dogs, with a certain alert swagger that reminded one of the walk of some light-weight prize-fighters. In fights with cougars, bears, and lynx, they too had been badly mauled and had lost a good many of their teeth. Neither of the gallant little fellows survived the trip. Their place as taken by a white bulldog bitch, Queen, which we picked up at the Keyston Ranch; a very affectionate and good-humored dog, but, when her blood was aroused, a dauntless though rather stupid fighter. Unfortunately she did not seize by the head, taking hold of any part that was nearest.

The pack had many interesting peculiarities, but none more so than the fact that four of them climbed trees. Only one of the hounds, little Jimmie, ever tried the feat; but of the fighters, not only Tony and Baldy but big Turk climbed every tree that gave them any chance. The pinyons and cedars were low, multi-forked, and usually sent off branches from near the ground. In consequence the dogs could, by industrious effort, work their way almost to the top. Now and then a dog would lose his footing and come down with a whack which sounded as if he must be disabled, but after a growl and a shake he would start up the tree again. They could not fight well while in a tree, and were often scratched or knocked to the ground by a cougar; and when the quarry was shot out of its perch and seized by the expectant throng below, the dogs in the tree, yelping with eager excitement, dived headlong down through the branches, regardless of consequences.

The horses were stout, hardy, surefooted beasts, not very fast, but able to climb like goats, and to endure an immense amount of work. Goff and I each used two for the trip.

We rode in to the Keystone Ranch late on the evening of the second day after leaving Meeker. We had picked up a couple of bobcats on the way, and had found a cougar's kill (or bait, as Goff called it)—a doe, almost completely eaten. The dogs puzzled for several hours, over the cold trail of the cougar; but it was old, and ran hither and thither over bare ground, so that they finally lost it. The ranch was delightfully situated at the foot of high wooded hills broken by cliffs, and it was pleasant to reach the warm, comfortable log buildings, with their clean rooms, and to revel in the abundant, smoking-hot dinner, after the long, cold hours in the saddle. As everywhere else in the cattle country nowadays, a successful effort had been made to store water on the Keystone, and there were great stretches of wire fencing—two improvements entirely unknown in former days. But the foreman, William Wilson, and the two punchers or cowhands, Sabey and Collins, were of the old familiar type—skilled, fearless, hardy, hard-working, with all the intelligence and self-respect that we like to claim as typical of the American character at its best. All three carried short saddle guns when they went abroad, and killed a good many coyotes, and now and then a gray wolf. The cattle were for the most part grade Herefords, very different from the wild, slab-sided, long-horned creatures which covered the cattle country a score of years ago.

The next day, January 14th, we got our first cougar. This kind of hunting was totally different from that to which I had been accustomed. In the first place, there was no need of always being on the alert for a shot, as it was the dogs who did the work. In the next place, instead of continually scanning the landscape, what we had to do was to look down so as to be sure not to pass over any tracks; for frequently a cold trail would be indicated so faintly that the dogs themselves might pass it by, if unassisted by Goff's keen eyes and thorough knowledge of the habits of the quarry. Finally, there was no object in making an early start, as what we expected to find was not the cougar, but the cougar's trail; moreover, the horses and dogs, tough though they were, could not stand more than a certain amount, and to ride from sunrise to sunset, day in and day out, for five weeks just about tested the limits of their endurance.

We made our way slowly up the snow-covered pinyon-clad side of the mountain back of the house, and found a very old cougar trail which it was useless to try to run, and a couple of fresh bobcat trails which it was difficult to prevent the dogs from following. After criss-crossing over the shoulders of this mountain for two or three hours, and scrambling in and out of the ravines, we finally struck another cougar trail, much more recent, probably made thirty-six hours before. The hounds had been hunting free to one side or the other of our path. With a wave of Goff's hand away they went on the trail. Had it been fresh they would have run out of hearing at once, for it was fearfully rough country. But they were able to work but slowly along the loops and zigzags of the trail, where it led across bare spaces, and we could keep well in sight and hearing of them. Finally they came to where it descended the sheer side of the mountain and crossed the snow-covered valley beneath. They were still all together, the pace having been so slow, and in the snow of the alley the scent was fresh. It was a fine sight to see them as they rushed across from one side to the other, the cliffs echoing their chiming. Jim and the three bitches were in the lead, while Boxer fell behind, as he always did when the pace was fast.

Leading our horses, we slid and scrambled after the hounds; but when we reached the valley they had passed out of sight and sound, and we did not hear them again until we had toiled up the mountain opposite. They were then evidently scattered, having come upon many bare places; but while we were listening, and working our way over to the other side of the divide, the sudden increase in the baying told Goff that they had struck the fresh trail of the beast they were after; and in two or three minutes we head Jim's deep voice "barking treed." The three fighters, who had been trotting at our heels, recognized the difference in the sound quite as quickly as we did, and plunged at full speed toward it down the steep hillside, throwing up the snow like so many snow-ploughs. In a minute or two the chorus told us that all the dogs were around the tree, and we picked our way down toward them.

While we were still some distance off we could see the cougar in a low pinyon, moving about as the dogs tried to get up, and finally knocking one clean out of the top. It was the first time I had ever seen dogs with a cougar, and I was immensely interested. The cougar, not liking the sight of the reinforcements, jumped out. She came down just outside the pack and ran uphill. So quick was she that the dogs failed to seize her, and for the first fifty yards she went a great deal faster than they did. Both in the jump and in the run she held her tail straight out behind her; I found out afterward that sometimes one will throw its tail straight in the air, and when walking along, when first roused by the pack, before they are close, will, if angry, lash the tail from side to side, at the same time grinning and snarling.

In a minute the cougar went up another tree, but as we approached, again jumped down, and on this occasion, after running a couple of hundred yards, the dogs seized it. The worry was terrific; the growling, snarling, and yelling rang among the rocks; and leaving our horses we plunged at full speed through the snow down the rugged ravine in which the fight was going on. It was a small though old female, only a few pounds heavier than either Turk or Jim, and the dogs had the upper hand when we arrived. They would certainly have killed it unassisted, but as it was doing some damage to the pack, and might at any moment kill a dog, I ended the struggle by a knife-thrust behind the shoulder. To shoot would have been quite as dangerous for the dogs as for their quarry. Three of the dogs were badly scratched, and Turk had been bitten through one foreleg, and Boxer through on hind leg.

The fighting dogs were the ones that enabled me to

use the knife. All three went straight for the head, and when they got hold they kept their jaws shut, worrying and pulling, and completely absorbing the attention of the cougar, so as to give an easy chance for the death-blow. The hounds meanwhile had seized the cougar behind, and Jim, with his alligator jaws, probably did as much damage as Turk. However, neither in this nor in any other instance, did any one of the dogs manage to get its teeth through the thick skin. When cougars fight among themselves their claws and fangs leave great scars, but their hides are too thick for the dogs to get their teeth through. On the other hand, a cougar's jaws have great power, and dogs are frequently killed by a single bite, the fangs being driven through the brain or spine; or they break a dog's leg or cut the big blood-vessels of the throat.

We weighed and measured the cougar, and then took lunch, making as impartial a distribution of it as was possible among ourselves and the different members of the pack; for, of course, we were already growing to have a hearty fellow-feeding for each individual dog.

The dogs were a source of unceasing amusement, not merely while hunting, but because of their relations to one another when off duty. Queen's temper was of the shortest toward the rest of the pack, although, like Turk, she was fond of literally crawling into my lap, when we sat down to rest after the worry which closed the chase. As soon as I began to eat my lunch, all the dogs clustered close around and I distributed small morsels to each in turn. Once Jimmie, Queen, and Boxer were sitting side by side, tightly wedged together. I treated them with entire impartiality; and soon Queen's feelings overcame her, and she unostentatiously but firmly bit Jimmie in the jaw.

Jimmie howled tremendously and Boxer literally turned a back somersault, evidently fearing lest his turn should come next.

Next morning we started early, intending to go to Juniper Mountain, where we had heard that cougars were plentiful; but we had only ridden about half an hour from the ranch when we came across a trail which by the size we knew must belong to an old male. It was about thirty-six hours old and led into a tangle of bad lands where there was great difficulty in working it out. Finally however, we found where it left these bad lands and went straight up a mountain-side, too steep for the horses to follow. From the plains below we watched the hounds working to and fro until they entered a patch of pinyons in which we were certain the cougar had killed a deer, as ravens and magpies were sitting around in the trees. In these pinyons the hounds were again at fault for a little while, but at last evidently found the right trail, and followed it up over the hill-crest and out of sight. We then galloped hard along the plain to the left, going around the end of the ridge and turning to our right on the other side. Here we entered a deep narrow valley or gorge which led up to a high plateau at the farther end. On our right, as we rode up the valley, lay the high and steep ridge over which the hounds had followed the trail. On the left it was still steeper, the slope being broken by ledges and precipices. Near the mouth of the gorge we encountered the hounds, who had worked the trail down and across the gorge, and were now hunting up the steep cliff-shoulder to our left. Evidently the cougar had wandered to and fro over his shoulder, and the dogs were much puzzled and worked in zigzags and circles around it, gradually getting clear to the top. Then old Boxer suddenly gave tongue with renewed zest and started off at a run almost on top of the ridge, the other dogs following. Immediately afterward they jumped the cougar.

We had been waiting below to see which direction the chase would take and now put spurs to our horses and galloped up the ravine, climbing the hillside on our right so as to get a better view of what was happening. A few hundred yards of this galloping and climbing brought us again in sight of the hounds. They were now barking treed and were clustered around a pinyon below the ridge crest on the side hill opposite us. Turk and Queen, who had been following at our horses' heels, appreciated what had happened as soon as we did, and leaving us, ran down into the valley and began to work their way through the deep snow up the hillside opposite toward where the hounds were. Ours was an ideal position for seeing the whole chase. In a minute the cougar jumped out of the tree down among the hounds, who made no attempt to seize him, but followed him as soon as he had cleared their circle. He came down hill at a great rate and jumped over a low cliff, bringing after him such an avalanche of snow that it was a moment before I caught sight of him again, this time crouched on a narrow ledge some fifteen or twenty feet below the brink from which he had jumped, and about as far above the foot of the cliff, where the steep hill-slope again began. The hounds soon found him and came along the ledge barking loudly, but not venturing near where he lay facing them, with his back arched like a great cat. Turk and Queen were meanwhile working their way up hill. Turk got directly under the ledge and could not find a way up. Queen went to the left and in a minute we saw her white form as she made her way through the dark-colored hounds straight for the cougar.

"That's the end of Queen," said Goff; "he'll kill her now, sure." In another moment she had made her rush and the cougar, bounding forward, had seized her, and as we afterward discovered had driven his great fangs right through the side of her head, fortunately missing the brain. In the struggle he lost his footing and rolled off the ledge, and when they struck the ground below he let go of the bitch. Turk, who was near where they struck, was not able to spring for the hold he desired, and in another moment the cougar was coming down hill like a quarter horse. We stayed perfectly still, as he was traveling in our direction. Queen was on her feet almost as quick as the cougar, and she and Turk tore after him, the hounds following in a few seconds, being delayed in getting off the ledge. It was astounding to see the speed of the cougar. He ran considerably more than a quarter of a mile down hill, and at the end of it had left the dogs more than a hundred yards behind. But his bolt was shot, and after going perhaps a hundred yards or so up the hill on our side and below us, he climbed a tree, under which the dogs began to bay frantically, while we scrambled toward them. When I got down I found him standing half upright on a big branch, his forepaws hung over another higher branch, his sides puffing like bellows, and evidently completely winded. In scrambling up the pinyon he must have struck a patch of resin, for it had torn a handful of hair off from behind his right forearm. I shot him through the heart. At the shot he sprang clean into the top of the tree, head and tail up, and his face fairly demonic with rage; but before he touched the ground he was dead. Turk jumped up, sized him as he fell, and the two rolled over a low ledge, falling about eight feet into the snow, Turk never losing his hold.

No one could have wished to see a prettier chase under better circumstances. It was exceedingly interesting. The only dog hurt was Queen, and very miserable indeed she looked. She stood in the trail, refusing to lie down or to join the other dogs, as, with prodigious snarls at one another, they ate the pieces of carcass we cut out for them. Dogs hunting every day, as these were doing, and going through such terrific exertion, need enormous quantities of meat, and as old horses and crippled steer were not always easy to get, we usually fed the cougar carcasses. On this occasion, when they had eaten until they could eat no longer, I gave most of my lunch to Queen—Boxer, who after his feast could hardly move, nevertheless waddling up with his ears forward to beg a share. Queen evidently felt that the lunch was a delicacy, for she ate it, and then trotted home behind us with the rest of the dogs. Rather to my astonishment, next day she was all right, and as eager to go with us as ever. Though one side of her head was much swollen, in her work she showed no signs of her injuries. The next day Goff and I cantered thirty miles into Meeker, and my holiday was over.

Rex

By D.H. Lawrence

From *Phoenix* by D.H. Lawrence.
Copyright 1936 by Freida Lawrence.
Permission of Viking Press.

D.H. Lawrence was an English writer whose experimental style, and obsession with the conflicts and relationships between men and women won him critical acclaim for such books as Sons and Lovers *and* Lady Chatterley's Lover, *and short stories such as* "The Rocking Horse Winner." *He became a cult figure in certain literary circles, and remains one to this day.*

When someone has loved, and been loved, by a dog and Death's scythe cuts his life away from his master's, it leaves a gaping wound. It never heals—as was the case for Lawrence, when he lost Rex.

Since every family has its black sheep, it almost follows that every man must have a sooty uncle. Lucky if he hasn't two. However, it is only with my mother's brother that we are concerned. She had loved him dearly when he was a little blond boy. When he grew up black, she was always vowing she would never speak to him again. Yet when he put in an appearance, after years of absence, she invariably received him in a festive mood, and was even flirty with him.

He rolled up one day in a dog-cart, when I was a small boy. He was large and bullet-headed and blustering, and this time, sporty. Sometimes he was rather literary, sometimes colored with business. But this time he was in checks, and was sporty. We viewed him from a distance.

The upshot was, would we rear a pup for him. Now my mother detested animals about the house. She could not bear the mix-up of human with animal life. Yet she consented to bring up the pup.

My uncle had taken a large, vulgar public house in a large and vulgar town. It came to pass that I must fetch the pup. Strange for me, a member of the Band of Hope, to enter the big, noisy smelly plate-glass-and-mahogany public house. It was The Good Omen. Strange to have my uncle towering over me in the passage, shouting, "Hello, Johnny, what do you want?" He didn't know me. Strange to think he was my mother's brother, and that he had his bouts when he read Browning aloud with emotion and éclat.

I was given tea in a narrow, uncomfortable sort of living room, half kitchen. Curious that such a palatial pub should show such miserable private accommodations, but so it was. There was I, unhappy, and glad to escape with the soft, fat pup. It was wintertime, and I wore a big-flapped black overcoat, half cloak. Under the cloak-sleeves I hid the puppy, who trembled. It was Saturday, and the train was crowded, and he whimpered under my coat. I sat in mortal fear of being hauled out for traveling without a dog-ticket. However, we arrived, and my torments were for nothing.

The others were wildly excited over the puppy. He was small and fat and white, with a brown-and-black head: a fox terrier. My father said he had a lemon head—some such mysterious technical phraseology. It wasn't lemon at all, but colored like a field bee. And he had a black spot at the root of his spine.

It was Saturday night—bath-night. He crawled on the hearth rug like a fat white teacup, and licked the bare toes that had just been bathed.

"He ought to be called Spot," said one. But that was too ordinary. It was a great question, what to call him.

"Call him Rex the King," said my mother, looking down on the fat, animated little teacup, who was chewing my sister's little toe and making her squeal with joy and tickles. We took the name in all seriousness.

"Rex—the King!" We thought it was just right. Not for years did I realize that it was sarcasm on my mother's part. She must have wasted some twenty years or more of irony on our incurable naïveté.

It wasn't a successful name, really. Because my father, and all the people in the street failed completely to pronounce the monosyllable Rex. They all said Rax. And it always distressed me. It always suggested to me seaweed, and rack-and-ruin. Poor Rex.

We loved him dearly. The first night we woke to hear

him weeping and whining in loneliness at the foot of the stairs. When it could be borne no more, I slipped down for him, and he slept under the sheets.

"I won't have that little beast in the beds. Beds are not for dogs," declared my mother callously.

"He's as good as we are!" we cried, injured.

"Whether he is or not, he's not going in the beds."

I think now, my mother scorned us for our lack of pride. We were a little *infra dig.*, we children.

The second night, however, Rex wept the same and in the same way was comforted. The third night we heard our father plod downstairs, heard several slaps administered to the yelping, dismayed puppy, and heard the amiable, but to us heartless voice saying, "Shut it then! Shut thy noise, 'st hear? Stop in thy basket, stop there!"

"It's a shame!" we shouted, in muffled rebellion, from the sheets.

"I'll give you shame, if you don't hold your noise and go to sleep," called our mother from her room. Whereupon we shed angry tears and went to sleep. But there was a tension.

"Such a houseful of idiots would make me detest the little beast, even if he was better than he is," said my mother.

But as a matter of fact she did not detest Rexie at all. She only had to pretend to do so, to balance our adoration. And in truth, she did not care for close contact with animals. She was too fastidious. My father, however, would take on a real dog's voice, talking to the puppy: a funny, high, singsong falsetto which he seemed to produce at the top of his head, " 'S a pretty little dog! 'S a pretty little doggy! Ay! Yes! Wag thy strunt then! Wag thy strunt,

Raxie!—Ha-ha! Nay, tha munna…" This last as the puppy, wild with excitement at the strange falsetto voice, licked my father's nostrils and bit my father's nose with his sharp little teeth. "He makes blood come," said my father.

"Serves you right for being so silly with him," said my mother. It was odd to see her as she watched the man, my father, crouching and talking to the little dog and laughing strangely when the little creature bit his nose and tousled his beard. What does a woman think of her husband at such a moment?

My mother amused herself over the names we called him.

"He's an angel—he's a little butterfly—Rexie, my sweet!"

"Sweet! A dirty little object!" interpolated my mother. She and he had a feud from the first. Of course he chewed boots and worried our stockings and swallowed our garters. The moment we took off our stockings he would dart away with one, we after him. Then as he hung, growling vociferously, at one end of the stocking, we at the other, we would cry:

"Look at him, Mother! He'll make holes in it again." Whereupon my mother darted at him and spanked him sharply.

"Let go, sir, you destructive little fiend!"

But he didn't let go. He began to growl with real rage, and hung on viciously. Mite as he was, he defied her with a manly fury. He did not hate her, nor she him. But they had one long battle with one another.

"I'll teach you, my Jockey! Do you think I'm going to spend my life darning after your destructive little teeth! I'll show you if I will!"

But Rexie only growled more viciously. They both became really angry, whilst we children expostulated earnestly with both. He would not let her take the stocking from him.

"You should tell him properly, Mother. He won't be driven," we said.

"I'll drive him further than he bargains for. I'll drive him out of my sight forever, that I will," declared my mother, truly angry. He would put her into a real temper, with his tiny, growling defiance.

"He's sweet! A Rexie, a little Rexie!"

"A filthy little nuisance! Don't think I'll put up with him."

And to tell the truth, he was dirty at first. How could he be otherwise, so young! But my mother hated him for it. For he lived in the house with us. He would wrinkle his nose and show his tiny dagger-teeth in fury when he was thwarted, and his growls of real battle-rage against my mother rejoiced us as much as they angered her. But at last she caught him *in flagrante*. She pounced on him, rubbed his nose in the mess, and flung him out into the yard. He yelped with shame and disgust and indignation. I shall never forget the sight of him as he rolled over, then tried to turn his head away from the disgust of his own muzzle, shaking his little snout with a sort of horror, and trying to sneeze it off. My sister gave a yell of despair, and dashed out with a rag and a pan of water, weeping wildly. She sat in the middle of the yard with the befouled puppy, and shedding bitter tears she wiped him and washed him clean. Loudly she reproached my mother. "Look how much bigger you are than he is. It's a shame, it's a shame!"

"You ridiculous little lunatic, you've undone all the

good it would do him, with your soft ways. Why is my life made a curse with animals! Haven't I enough as it is…"

There was subdued tension afterward. Rex was a little white chasm between us and our parent.

He became clean. But then another tragedy loomed. He must be docked. His floating puppy-tail must be docked short. This time my father was the enemy. My mother agreed with us that is was an unnecessary cruelty. But my father was adamant. "The dog'll look a fool all his life, if he's not docked." And there was no getting away from it. To add to the horror, poor Rex's tail must be bitten off. Why bitten? we asked aghast. We were assured that biting was the only way. A man would take the little tail and just nip it through with his teeth at a certain point. My father lifted his lips and bared his incisors, to suit the description. We shuddered. But we were in the hands of fate.

Rex was carried away, and a man called Rowbotham bit off the superfluity of his tail in the Nags Head, for a quart of best and bitter. We lamented our poor diminished puppy, but agreed to find him more manly and *comme il faut*. We should always have been ashamed of his little whip of a tail, if it had not been shortened. My father said it had made a man out of him.

Perhaps it had. For now his true nature came out. And his true nature, like so much else, was dual. First he was a fierce, canine little beast, a beast of rapine and blood. He longed to hunt savagely. He lusted to set his teeth in his prey. It was no joke with him. The old canine Adam stood first in him, the dog with fangs and glaring eyes. He flew at us when we annoyed him. He flew at all intruders, particularly the postman. He was almost a peril to the neighborhood. But not quite. Because close second in his nature stood that fatal need to love, the *besoin d'aimer* which at last makes an end of liberty. He had a terrible, terrible necessity to love, and this trammelled the native, savage hunting beast which he was. He was torn between two great impulses: the native impulse to hunt and kill, and the strange, secondary, supervening impulse to love and obey. If he had been left to my father and mother, he would have run wild and got himself shot. As it was, he loved us children with a fierce, joyous love. And we loved him.

When we came home from school we would see him standing at the end of the entry, cocking his head wistfully at the open country in front of him, and meditating whether to be off or not: a white, inquiring little figure, with green savage freedom in front of him. A cry from a far distance from one of us, and like a bullet he hurled himself down the road, in a mad game. Seeing him coming, my sister invariably turned and fled, shrieking with delighted terror. And he would leap straight up her back, and bite her and tear her clothes. But it was only an ecstasy of savage love, and she knew it. She didn't care if he tore her pinafores. But my mother did.

My mother was maddened by him. He was a little demon. At the least provocation, he flew. You had only to sweep the floor, and he bristled and sprang at the broom. Nor would he let go. With his scruff erect and his nostrils snorting rage, he would turn up the whites of his eyes at my mother, as she wrestled at the other end of the broom. "Leave go, sir; leave go!" she wrestled and stamped her foot, and he answered with horrid growls. In the end it was she who had to let go. Then she flew at him, and he flew at her. All the time we had him he was within a hair's-breadth of savagely biting her. And she knew it. Yet he always kept sufficient self-control.

We children loved his temper. We would drag the bones from his mouth, and put him into such paroxysms of rage that he would twist his head right over and lay it on the ground upside-down, because he didn't know what to do with himself, the savage was so strong in him and he must fly at us. "He'll fly at your throat one of these days," said my father. "Neither he nor my mother dared touch Rex's bone. It was enough to see him bristle and roll the whites of his eyes when they came near. How near he must have been to driving his teeth right into us, cannot be told. He was a horrid sight, snarling and crouching at us. But we only laughed and rebuked him. And he would whimper in the sheer torment of his need to attack us.

He never did hurt us. He never hurt anybody, though the neighborhood was terrified of him. But he took to hunting. To my mother's disgust, he would bring large, dead, bleeding rats and lay them on the hearth rug, and she had to take them up on a shovel. For he would not remove them. Occasionally he brought a mangled rabbit, and sometimes, alas, fragmentary poultry. We were in terror of prosecution. Once he came home bloody and feathery and rather sheepish-looking. We cleaned him and questioned him and abused him. Next day we heard of six dead ducks. Thank heaven no one had seen him.

But he was disobedient. If he saw a hen he was off, and calling would not bring him back. He was worst of all with my father, who would take him for walks on Sunday mornings. My mother would not walk a yard with him. Once, walking with my father, he rushed off at some sheep, and meant business. My father crawled through the hedge, and was upon him in time. And now the man was in a paroxysm of rage. He dragged the little beast into the road and thrashed him with a walking stick.

"Do you know you're thrashing that dog unmercifully?" said a passerby.

"Ay, an' mean to," shouted my father.

The curious thing was that Rex did not respect my father any the more for the beatings he had from him. He took much more heed of us children, always.

But he let us down also. One fatal Saturday he disappeared. We hunted and called, but no Rex. We were bathed, and it was bedtime, but we would not go to bed. Instead we sat in a row in our nightdresses on the sofa, and wept without stopping. This drove our mother mad.

"Am I going to put up with it? Am I? And for all that hateful little beast of a dog! He shall go! If he's not gone now, he shall go."

Our father came in late, looking rather queer, with his hat over his eye. But in his staccato, tippled fashion he tried to be consoling.

"Never mind, my duckie, I shall look for him in the morning."

Sunday came—oh, such a Sunday. We cried, and didn't eat. We scoured the land, and for the first time realized how empty and wide the earth is, when you're looking for something. My father walked for many miles—all in vain. Sunday dinner, with rhubarb pudding. I remember, and an atmosphere of abject misery that was unbearable.

"Never," said my mother, "never shall an animal set foot in this house again while I live. I knew what it would be! I knew."

The day wore on, and it was the black gloom of bed-time when we heard a scratch and an impudent little whine at the door. In trotted Rex, mud-black, disreputable, and impudent. His air of off-hand "how d'ye do!" was inde-scribable. He trotted round with suffisance, wagging his tail as if to say, "Yes, I've come back. But I didn't need to. I can carry on remarkably well by myself." Then he walked into his water and drank noisily and ostentatiously. It was rather a slap in the eye for us.

He disappeared once or twice in this fashion. We never knew where he went. And we began to feel that his heart was not so golden as we had imagined it.

But one fatal day reappeared my uncle and the dog-cart. He whistled to Rex, and Rex trotted up. But when he wanted to examine the lusty, sturdy dog, Rex became suddenly still, then sprang free. Quite jauntily he trotted round—but out of reach of my uncle. He leaped up, lick-ing our faces, and trying to make us play.

"Why what have you done with the dog—you've made a fool of him. He's softer than grease. You've ruined him. You've made a fool of him," shouted my uncle.

Rex was captured and hauled off to the dog-cart and tied to the seat. He was in a frenzy. He yelped and shrieked and struggled, and was hit on the head, hard with the butt-end of my uncle's whip, which only made him struggle more frantically. So we saw him driven away, our beloved Rex, frantically, madly fighting to get to us from the high dog-cart, and being knocked down, while we stood in the street in mute despair.

After which, black tears, and a little wound which is still alive in our hearts.

I saw Rex only once again, when I had to call just once

at The Good Omen. He must have heard my voice, for he was upon me in the passage before I knew where I was. And in the instant I knew how he loved us. He really loved us. And in the same instant there was my uncle with a whip, beating and kicking him back, and Rex cowering, bristling, snarling.

My uncle swore many oaths, how we had ruined the dog for ever, made him vicious, spoiled him for showing purposes, and been altogether a pack of mard-soft fools not fit to be trusted with any dog but a gutter-mongrel.

Poor Rex! We heard his temper was incurably vicious, and he had to be shot.

And it was our fault. We had loved him too much, and he had loved us too much. We never had another pet.

It is a strange thing, love. Nothing but love has made the dog lose his wild freedom, to become the servant of man. And his very servility or completeness of love makes a term of deepest contempt—"Your dog!"

We should not have loved Rex so much, and he should not have loved us. There should have been a measure. We tended, all of us, to overstep the limits of our own natures. He should have stayed outside human limits; we should have stayed outside canine. Nothing is more fatal than the disaster of too much love. My uncle was right, we had ruined the dog.

My uncle was a fool, for all that.

The Road to Tinkhamtown

By Corey Ford

With kind thanks to Dartmouth College for permission to
reprint for the first time anywhere, the complete original
version of this beloved story, which is considered by many
to be the greatest outdoor story ever written.
From his original manuscript, copied by Laurie Morrow.

The road was long, but he knew where he was going. He would follow the old road through the swamp and up over the ridge and down to a deep ravine, and cross the sagging timbers of the bridge, and on the other side would be the place called Tinkhamtown. He was going back to Tinkhamtown.

He walked slowly, for his legs were dragging, and he had not been walking for a long time. He had not walked for almost a year, and his flanks had shriveled and wasted away from lying in bed so long; he could fit his fingers around his thigh. Doc Towle had said he would never walk again, but that was Doc for you, always on the pessimistic side. Why, here he was walking quite easily, once he had started. The strength was coming back into his legs, and he did not have to stop for breath so often. He tried jogging a few steps, just to show he could, but he slowed again because he had a long way to go.

It was hard to make out the old road, choked with young alders and drifted over with matted leaves, and he shut his eyes so he could see it better. He could always see it whenever he shut his eyes. Yes, here was the beaver dam on the right, just as he remembered it, and the flooded stretch where he had to wade, picking his way from hummock to hummock while the dog splashed unconcernedly in front of him. The water had been over his boot tops in one place, and sure enough as he waded it now, his left boot filled with water again, the same warm, squidgy feeling. Everything was the way it had been that afternoon. Nothing had changed. Here was the blowdown across the road that he had clambered over and here on a knoll was the clump of thorn apples where Cider had put up a grouse—he remembered the sudden roar as the grouse thundered out, and the easy shot that he missed—they had not taken time to go after it. Cider had wanted to look for it, but he had whistled him back. They were looking for Tinkhamtown.

Everything was the way he remembered. There was a fork in the road, and he halted and felt in the pocket of his hunting coat and took out the map he had drawn twenty years ago. He had copied it from a chart he found in the Town Hall, rolled up in a cardboard cylinder covered with dust. He used to study the old survey charts; sometimes they showed where a farming community had flourished once, and around the abandoned pastures and under the apple trees, grown up to pine, the grouse would be feeding undisturbed. Some of his best grouse-covers had been located that way. The chart had crackled with age as he unrolled it; the date was 1847. It was the sector between Kearsarge and Cardigan Mountains, a wasteland of slash and second-growth timber without habitation today, but evidently it had supported a number of families before the Civil War. A road was marked on the map, dotted with X's for homesteads and the names of the owners were lettered beside them: Nason, J. Tinkham, Libbey, Allard, R. Tinkham. Half the names were Tinkham. In the center of the map—the paper was so yellow he could barely make it out—was the word Tinkhamtown.

He copied the chart carefully, noting where the road turned off at the base of Kearsarge and ran north and then northeast and crossed a brook that was not even named on the chart; and early the next morning he and Cider had set out together to find the place. They could not drive very far in the jeep, because washouts had gutted the roadbed and laid bare the ledges and boulders, like a stream bed.

He had stuffed the sketch in his hunting-coat pocket, and hung his shotgun over his forearm and started walking, the old setter trotting ahead of him, with the bell on his collar tinkling. It was an old-fashioned sleighbell, and it had a thin silvery note that echoed through the woods like peepers in the spring; he could follow the sound in the thickest cover, and when it stopped, he would go to where he heard it last and Cider would be on point. After Cider's death, he had put the bell away. He'd never had another dog.

It was silent in the woods without the bell, and the way was longer than he remembered. He should have come to the big hill by now. Maybe he'd taken the wrong turn back at the fork. He thrust a hand into his hunting-coat; the sketch he had drawn was still in the pocket. He sat down on a flat rock to get his bearings, and then he realized, with a surge of excitement, that he had stopped for lunch on this very rock ten years ago. Here was the waxed paper from his sandwich, tucked in a crevice, and here was the hollow in the leaves where Cider had stretched out bedside him, the dog's soft muzzle flattened on his thighs. He looked up, and through the trees he could see the hill.

He rose and started walking again, carrying his shotgun. He had left the gun standing in its rack in the kitchen, when he had been taken to the state hospital, but now it was hooked over his arm by the trigger guard; he could feel the solid heft of it. The woods were more dense as he climbed, but here and there a shaft of sunlight slanted through the trees. "And the forests ancient as the hills," he thought, "enfolding sunny spots of greenery."

Funny that should come back to him now; he hadn't read it since he was a boy. Other things were coming back to him, the smell of the dank leaves and sweetfern and frosted apples, the sharp contrast of sun and the cool November shade, the stillness before snow. He walked faster, feeling the excitement swell within him.

He had walked all that morning, stopping now and then to study the map and take his bearings from the sun, and the road that led them down a long hill and at the bottom was the brook he had seen on the chart, a deep ravine spanned by a wooden bridge. Cider had trotted across the bridge, and he had followed more cautiously, avoiding the loose planks and walking the solid struts with his shotgun held out to balance himself; and that was how he found Tinkhamtown.

On the other side of the brook was a clearing, he remembered, and the remains of a stone wall, and a cellar-hole, where a farmhouse had stood. Cider had moved in a long cast around the edge of the clearing, his bell tinkling faintly, and he had paused a moment beside the foundations, wondering about the people who had lived here a century ago. Had they ever come back to Tinkhamtown? And then suddenly the bell had stopped, and he had hurried across the clearing. An apple tree was growing in a corner of the stone wall, and under the tree Cider had halted at point. He could see it all now: the warm October sunlight, the ground strewn with freshly-pecked apples, the dog standing immobile with one foreleg drawn up, his back level and his tail a white plume. Only his flanks quivered a little, and a string of slobber dangled from his jowls. "Steady, boy," he murmured as he moved up behind him, I'm coming."

He paused on the crest of the hill, straining his ears for the faint mutter of the stream below him, but he could not hear it because of the voices. He wished they would stop talking, so he could hear the stream. Someone was saying his name over and over. Someone said "What is it, Frank?" and he opened his eyes. Doc Towle was standing at the foot of the bed, whispering to the new nurse, Mrs. Simmons or something; she'd only been here a few days, but Doc thought it would take some of the burden off his wife. He turned his head on the pillow, and looked up at his wife's face, bent over him. "What did you say, Frank?" she asked, and her face was worried. Why, there was nothing to be worried about. He wanted to tell her where he was going, but when he moved his lips no sound came. "What?" she asked, bending her head lower. "I don't hear you." He couldn't make the words any clearer, and she straightened and said to Doc Towle: "It sounded something like Tinkhamtown."

"Tinkhamtown?" Doc shook his head. "Never heard him mention any place by that name."

He smiled to himself. Of course he'd never mentioned it to Doc. There are some things you don't mention even to an old hunting companion like Doc. Things like a secret grouse cover you didn't mention to anyone, not even to as close a friend as Doc was. No, he and Cider were the only ones who knew. They had found it together, that long ago afternoon, and it was their secret. "This is our secret cover," he had told Cider that afternoon, as he lay sprawled under the tree with the grouse beside him and the dog's muzzle flattened on his thigh. "Just you and me." He had never told anybody else about Tinkhamtown, and he had never gone back after Cider died.

"Better let him rest," he heard Doc tell his wife. It was funny to hear them talking, and not be able to make them hear him. "Call me if there's any change."

The old road lay ahead of him, dappled with sunshine. He could smell the dank leaves, and feel the chill of the shadows under the hemlocks; it was more real than the pain in his legs. Sometimes it was hard to tell what was real and what was something he remembered. Sometimes at night he would hear Cider panting on the floor beside his bed, his toenails scratching as he chased a bird in a dream, but when the nurse turned on the light the room would be empty. And then when it was dark he would hear the panting and scratching again.

Once he asked Doc point blank about his legs. "Will they ever get better?" He and Doc had grown up in town together; they knew each other too well to lie. Doc had shifted his big frame in the chair beside the bed, and got out his pipe and fumbled with it, and looked at him. "No, I'm afraid not," he replied slowly, "I'm afraid there's nothing to do." Nothing to do but lie here and wait till it's over. Nothing to do but lie here like this, and be waited on, and be a burden to everybody. He had a little insurance, and his son in California sent what he could to help, but now with the added expense of a nurse and all... "Tell me, Doc," he whispered, for his voice wasn't as strong these days, "what happens when it's over?" And Doc put away the needle and fumbled with the catch of his black bag and said he supposed that you went on to someplace else called the Hereafter. But he shook his head; he always argued with Doc. "No," he told him, "it isn't someplace else. It's someplace you've been where you want to be again, someplace you were happiest." Doc didn't understand, and he couldn't explain it any better. He knew what he meant, but the shot was taking effect and he was tired. The pain had been worse lately, and Doc had started giving him shots with a needle so he could sleep. But he didn't really sleep, because the memories kept coming back to him, or maybe he kept going back to the memories.

He was tired now, and his legs ached a little as he started down the hill toward the stream. He could not see the road; it was too dark under the trees to see the sketch he had drawn. The trunks of all the trees were swollen with moss, and blowdowns blocked his way and he had to circle around their upended roots, black and misshapen. He had no idea which way Tinkhamtown was, and he was frightened. He floundered into a pile of slash, feeling the branches tear at his legs as his boots sank in, and he did not have the strength to get through it and he had to back out again, up the hill. He did not know where he was going any more.

He listened for the stream, but all he could hear was his wife, her breath catching now and then in a dry sob. She wanted him to come back, and Doc wanted him to, and there was the big house. If he left the house alone, it would fall in with the snow and cottonwoods would grow in the cellar hole. There were all the other doubts, but most of all there was the fear. He was afraid of the darkness and being alone, and not knowing the way. He had lost the way. Maybe he should turn back. It was late, but maybe, maybe he could find the way back.

He paused on the crest of the hill, straining his ears for the faint mutter of the stream below him, but he could not hear it because of the voices. He wished they would stop talking, so he could hear the stream. Someone was saying his name over and over.

They had come to the stream—he shut his eyes so he could see it again—and Cider had trotted across the bridge. He had followed more cautiously, avoiding the loose planks and walking on a beam, with his shotgun held out to balance himself. On the other side the road rose sharply to a level clearing and he paused beside the split-stone foundation of a house. The fallen timbers were rotting under a tangle of briars and burdock, and in the empty cellar hole the cottonwoods grew higher than the house had been. His toe encountered a broken china cup and the rusted rims of a wagon wheel buried in the grass. Beside the granite doorsill was a lilac bush planted by the woman of the family to bring a touch of beauty to their home. Perhaps her husband had chided her for wasting time on such useless things, with as much work to be done. But all the work had come to nothing. The fruits of their work had disappeared, and still the lilac bloomed each spring, defying the encroaching forest, as though to prove that beauty is the only thing that lasts.

On the other side of the clearing were the sills of the barn, and behind it a crumbling stone wall around the orchard. He thought of the men sweating to clear the fields and pile the rocks into walls to hold their cattle. Why had they gone away from Tinkhamtown, leaving their walls to crumble and their buildings to collapse under the January snows? Had they ever come back to Tinkhamtown? Or were they still here, watching him unseen, living in a past that was more real than the present. He stumbled over a block of granite, hidden by briars, part of the sill of the old barn. Once it had been a tight barn, warm with cattle steaming in their stalls and sweet with the barn odor of manure and hay and leather harness. It seemed as though it was more real to him than the bare foundation and the empty space above them. Doc used to argue that what's over is over, but he would insist Doc was wrong. Everything is the way it was, he'd tell Doc. The present always changes, but the past is always the way it was. You leave it, and go on to the present, but it is still there, waiting for you to come back to it.

He had been so wrapped up in his thoughts that he had not realized Cider's bell had stopped. He hurried across the clearing, holding his gun ready. In a corner of the stone wall an ancient apple tree had covered the ground with red fruit, and beneath it Cider was standing motionless. The white fan of his tail was lifted a little, his neck stretched forward, and one foreleg was cocked. His flanks were trembling, and a thin skein of drool hung from his jowls. The dog did not move as he approached, but he could see the brown eyes roll back until their whites showed, waiting for him. His throat grew tight, the way it always did when Cider was on point, and he swallowed hard. "Steady, boy," he whispered, "I'm coming."

He opened his eyes. His wife was standing beside his bed and his son was standing near her. He looked at his son. Why had he come all the way from California, he worried? He tried to speak, but there was no sound. "I think his lips moved just now. He's trying to whisper something," his wife's voice said. "I don't think he knows you," his wife said to his son. Maybe he didn't know him. Never had, really. He had never been close to his wife or his son. He did not open his eyes, because he was watching for the grouse to fly as he walked past Cider, but he knew Doc Towle was looking at him. "He's sleeping," Doc said after a moment. Maybe you better get some sleep yourself. A chair creaked, and he heard Doc's heavy footsteps cross the room. "Call me if there's any change,"

Doc said, and closed the door, and in the silence he could hear his wife sobbing beside him, her dress rustling regularly as she breathed. How could he tell her he wouldn't be alone? But he wasn't alone, not with Cider. He had closed off the other rooms and slept on a cot in the kitchen with the old dog curled on the floor by the stove, his claws scratching the linoleum as he chased a bird in a dream. He wasn't alone when he heard that. They were always together. There was a closeness between them that he did not feel for anyone else, his wife, his son, or even Doc. They could talk without words, and they could always find each other in the woods. He was lost without him. Cider was the kindest person he had ever known.

They never hunted together after Tinkhamtown. Cider had acted tired, walking back to the car that afternoon, and several times he sat down in the trail, panting hard. He had to carry him in his arms the last hundred yards to the jeep. It was hard to think he was gone.

And then he heard it, echoing through the air, a sound like peepers in the spring, the high silvery note of a bell. He started running toward it, following it down the hill. The pain was gone from his legs, it had never been there. He hurdled blowdowns, he leapt over fallen trunks, he put one fingertip on a pile of slash and floated over it like a bird. The sound filled his ears, louder than a thousand churchbells ringing, louder than all the heavenly choirs in the sky, as loud as the pounding of his heart. His eyes were blurred with tears, but he did not need to see. The fear was gone; he was not alone. He knew the way now. He knew where he was going.

He paused at the stream just for a moment. He heard men's voices. They were his hunting partners, Jim, Mac,

Dan, Woodie. And oh, what a day it was for sure, closeness and understanding and happiness, the little intimate things, the private jokes. He wanted to tell them he was happy; if they only knew how happy he was. He opened his eyes, but could not see the room any more. Everything else was bright with sunshine, but the room was dark.

The bell had stopped, and he closed his eyes and looked across the stream. The other side was basked in gold bright sunshine, and he could see the road rising steeply through the clearing in the woods, and the apple tree in a corner of the stone wall. Cider was standing motionless, the white fan of his tail lifted a little, his neck craned forward, one foreleg cocked. The whites of his eyes showed as he looked back, waiting for him.

"Steady," he called, "steady, boy." He started across the bridge. "I'm coming."

In the margins of his manuscript, in a linear scrawl that bears precious little resemblance to handwriting, are Corey's directions to Tinkhamtown, a place he knew well and loved better. All the landmarks are there: the old N—— family farm, the backroad from town that leads over M—— Hill to S—— Rock and across to the road to Tinkhamtown. It used to be the main road to M——, then north to the Notch. The furrows in the road run so deep that the forest floor has failed to reclaim it; now, soft brown earth peeks through fist-sized rocks that were laid, variously, by man and nature.

It's a wild, enchanted place, thick with ancient trees that twist and turn and twine around one another; the heartiest are the strangest of all. They grow in ways no tree was meant to: some have deformed trunks that run perfectly parallel to the ground for ten or twelve feet before bending, like a human joint, to soar straight up through a clearing to reach the sun and touch the sky.

You go just as Corey said—that is, if you're coming in from the south and west, headed northeast. The beaver pond is on low ground and a hub for animal wildlife. You can't keep your balance above the dam without slipping, and slopping mud into your boot. Lots of beaver, moose, deer—but no people; not for years.

The village lies beyond. You have to manage a steep bank on the north side of the beaver pond, then head back to the road. You'll know when you get to Tinkhamtown. Crumbling foundations peek through saplings and low growth that have strangled what was once pasture, but you get a clear sense of the place. It was once a thriving sheep and farming community. A stone-fenced enclosure stands in the center of the village. This was the village sheep pen, and rust stains on hand-hewn granite posts mark where iron latches and bolts kept the gate closed to keep in ewes and lambs. At the top of the road is the apple orchard, but trees now are gnarled and overgrown. Yet in the fall, they still, somehow, bear fruit, and the apples are sweet. Some are yellow, some red, but they're very small. The lilacs that Corey tells about do stand in the doorway of one foundation, and they still bloom in spring. There are bushes, with clusters of deep purple flowers, full and fragrant. Breathe their perfume—you get a sweet, sorrowful feeling, knowing Tinkhamtown was once so full of life and laughter and hard-working folk.

Their story is told in the cemetery. It's down the road, about a quarter-mile. Corey touches upon it, why they went away. Well, they went away because they couldn't stand any longer the utter heartbreak of burying their young, their spouses, their loved ones, their friends. It was smallpox, and it took just about everybody. A sapling has grown square between the granite gateposts into the cemetery, but you can get through, if you go sideways and aren't too heavy. Toward the back are seven headstones, in a row that time's disheveled, that mark a family. From left to right: two little children, then their mother, then two more children. The fifth child, a son, survived, and he lived to fight in France in the First World War; but he was killed there and was sent home to be buried, like the rest, by his father. The last marker—the one on the right—that's his, old Nat Williams.

Old Orion used to tell how, when he was a young man, he and his brother were going home along the road to Tinkhamtown in their horse and cart after a dance in S———. It was late, a full moon hung in a bright night sky. They came upon Nat Williams' place and Orion looked over to the barn—the one Corey describes. The barn door was open, and hanging from the rafters was old Nat. "Ain't that old Nat Williams hanging from the rafters?" Orion asked. "Ayuh," his brother replied. "Damned if it ain't. Giddee-yup, Margrit." Of course, they went back to town and got Carroll and the boys to come help them cut Nat down. They gave him a Christian burial, next to his kin. Old Nat Williams— he was the last to leave Tinkhamtown; and the only one who stayed. He became a sort of recluse. They say he wouldn't leave his family, even though they had to leave him. He lived a long time after his son was killed, but he went mad, finally, from the grief. He was a strong man to survive the grief as long as he did, but Nat Williams was a crusty old New Englander, and you know what they say about the natives hereabouts: They come from the same earth as our New Hampshire granite. Corey admired that.

Anyway, that's Tinkhamtown. That's where Corey went every opening day of grouse season, except when he was serving as a Lieutenant Colonel in the U.S. Air Corps during World War II. That would have been thirty opening days, more or less, and he never did go back after Cider died.

Corey died in 1969, and so did all the elm trees in our village, and down in Tinkhamtown, too. Summer before last, something remarkable happened. Thirty, forty feet up, bursting from the dead shafts of the old elms in Tinkhamtown, grew masses of clusters of young, green leaves. See for yourself. If you ever find your way to Tinkhamtown, get out your pocket knife, chip away some dead bark, and underneath you'll see the cambium layer of spongy, new growth. That summer, something else happened—for me, at least. I met Corey through his forgotten archives, and knew, then, that he should come back to life too, through his stories. Then I found his grave. I brought flowers from Tinkhamtown. The clock tower at Dartmouth struck twelve, and it was the day *of the 25th anniversary of Corey's death. You don't believe me? Then you won't believe the elms, but that's true, too. But if you believe nothing else, believe in Tinkhamtown. It's real. It's where Corey said it was all along. And he kept it in his heart, till the day he died.*